THE FLIGHT OF CONSCIOUSNESS

THE FLIGHT
OF CONSCIOUSNESS

———◆———

A Contemporary Map
for the Spiritual Journey

Richard Harvey

Ashgrove Publishing
London & Bath

CONTENTS

PART 3: THE HIGHER SELF / 79

PART 4: THE FLIGHT OF CONSCIOUSNESS / 127

For Nicky

PREFACE

The spiritual journey is the deepening into ourselves we make throughout our lives. It is the merging into the eternal, dancing stillness and peace at the centre of our being. It is the return to our real nature. Anyone who experiences the 'call' to their spiritual path – whether or not within established religion – and who chooses to follow the 'call', is on their spiritual journey.

Today the spiritual secrets are freely available. There is little mystery left. You can find Tantric scriptures, Sufi texts, Taoist stories and Kabbalistic teachings in high-street bookstores which, not that many years ago, stocked only the Bible and C.S.Lewis. But it is not enough to simply know, or have access to, secrets. The question for us today is, 'How do we discover and live our enlightenment?' and to do this we need to undertake the spiritual journey.

I have written this book to help the contemporary spiritual seeker to see through the confusion that the ready availability of spiritual knowledge has brought; to show how the spiritual journey unfolds, and to assist the seeker in living his or her enlightenment. This map – as secular as it is religious, as transcendent as it is ordinary, as human as it is divine – will help to develop your insight and enable and empower you to become your true self. Above all, I hope this book will support your own inner knowing, sharpen your intuitive guidance and help you to discover your deep wisdom.

In the West, we have never been comfortable with the idea of the guru, because of the overwhelming importance laid on our individuality. This, in fact, can be one of our great strengths in the spiritual search, for the Higher Self is the flowering of our individual humanity. We should follow our own hearts and not surrender to any outer authority – even if it is the word of God itself.

Hear thou even the little child, and from his words accept thou the Truth that goeth straight to thy heart. But reject all that doth not so go to thy heart – no matter how high the authority – yea, even though the lotus-born creator, Brahm, himself, be the speaker.[1]

Of the many ideas put forward in this book there are four to which I would like to draw your attention:

Essentially, there are three ways to God and the highest of these transcends the illusion of separateness.

The Higher Self is already here. There is nothing to seek, therefore the way itself is the way of no-seeking.

The individual is himself/herself divine. The spiritual path today is an individual path. The way to our divinity is through acceptance of our unique individuality

God is within – God is the Self.

The Flight of Consciousness consists of a model of ten stages. At times you will pursue individual stages, at times various combinations of stages and at other times you may find yourself returning to a stage in which something was missed or unfulfilled. For each of us the spiritual journey is individual and unique. There are as many ways to God as there are individuals.

Nevertheless, the stages in this book reflect a deep unity in our individual journeys. Here is the essence of the spiritual journey with individual accounts, anecdotes and experiences to clarify the essential aspects of that journey.

I have included some exercises at the back of the book and some suggestions for reading further into the themes of the ten stages. You will also find details of the quotes used in the text there. Where an inset passage has no reference number it is an original account, either from my own experience or someone else's.

I would like to thank my editor, Brad Thompson and Robin Campbell at Ashgrove Publishing as well as Dr. John Allison, Julie Kaloczi and my wife, Nicky Harvey for their invaluable help in the preparation of this book.

R.H.

INTRODUCTION

For some days I had been engaged in a communication exercise on a Tantric Buddhist retreat. Long spells of sitting meditation interspersed with slow walking gave way to successive forty-minute sessions in which we would pair up with someone, and sit opposite them, and on the strike of a bell ask, 'Tell me who you are?' When the bell struck again the other would ask the same question.

The question is, of course, maddening. Once you have exhausted your personal details – statistics, faults, virtues – and your interminable history, you scratch your head. You have been instructed to carry on responding and so you begin to face the knowledge that either there is no answer because no one is there or, if you are truly there, you do not know the answer. The question is a *koan* – it has no logical answer – it is designed to awaken you.

The teacher was waiting for me in his room. I walked slowly through the meadow towards the French windows that opened directly onto the fields. The warm summer wind cut swathes through the lush green field like a comb brushing a giant's head. I could hear the starlings wheeling low, just above me in the magnificent azure sky. The sun was warm on my skin and there was a refreshing breeze. As I approached, I smelt the musky aroma of incense coming from the room. I sat down and looked into his face, noticing his kind and alert features.

'Tell me who you are?' he said.

Now, when the teacher asked the question, I felt a fork in the road open up in my consciousness. My mind focused on a very clear and definite choice. I could trot out the same old, tired, unconvincing and dead material from the past, interspersed with a few remarks designed to win approval and make him think well of me and the progress I had made on my spiritual quest. All of this was well known to me. Alternatively, I could take a leap into the unknown, abandon the usual parameters and safety settings and simply not know. It felt life threatening and yet strangely familiar. I had, after all, been avoiding this moment all of my life. And here was my opportunity…

I do not know how it happened. I do not know what I said or for how long I spoke. I dimly remember seeing a bird flying by and the deep blue sky framed in the window. I remember not feeling separate from the bird, the sky or the teacher. My awareness flew with that of the bird... I remember feeling at one with existence... the self in me dissolved and I was released... I flew and I soared... I knew nothing and everything... I was consciousness flying in total freedom.

When I stopped speaking the teacher looked at me and said, 'Now you are teaching me'. We smiled at each other. He gave me a new question and I left to return to the group, who were sitting in pairs engaged in the communication exercise.

As I returned, I can remember my old self returning, beginning to take hold again, pulling me out of the glorious feeling of oneness with all things. I started to relish the achievement, the graduation to the new question. Just after I sat down, the bell rang out. I leaned forward and said proudly to my partner, 'I have a new question', and promptly found that I had forgotten it – at least, it was not so much that I had forgotten it, but more that the words were 'swimming' inside me and I was not able to pin them down nor arrange them into what felt like the right order to reflect their meaning. I approached the teacher, who had returned and was sitting overseeing the group.

'Would you tell me my new question again?' I asked him.

'Existence is only now. What is it?' he replied. As I was returning to my seat he called to me. I turned. His demeanour was a mixture of intense seriousness, light humour and complete detachment. He had recast my question.

'How is life fulfilled?' he said.

... flying, running and rejoicing... he is free and will not be bound...
Thomas à Kempis, *The Imitation of Christ*

———•••———

Sages say that the thought 'I' does not rise even in the least, alone is Self which is silence. That silent Self alone is God: Self alone is the individual soul. Self alone is this ancient world.
Ramana Maharshi

———•••———

This is the one god of this one man. This is his world, his pleroma, his divinity. In this world is man Abraxas, the creator and the destroyer of his own world. This Star is the god and the goal of man... To this one god man shall pray.
C.G.Jung, *Seven Sermons for the Dead*

· Part 1·

BEGINNING THE SPIRITUAL JOURNEY

SEEING YOURSELF AS YOU ARE

You have to ask yourself the question 'Who am I?' This investigation will lead in the end to the discovery of something within you, which is behind the mind. Solve that great problem and you will solve all the other problems.

Ramana Maharshi

There is a powerful impulse towards wholeness within each of us. We desire balance in our lives and peace within, but lose ourselves in the activity of life. By identifying with our achievements, we lose ourselves in 'doing' and forget what it is to 'be'. In our haste to reach our goals we lose touch with our centre – the place where we simply are. All the while getting further away from a sense of meaning and purpose, some of us discover that activity is not the answer, and we see that we are running from ourselves.

We are more than our bodies, more than our thoughts. We have the unique capacity for self-awareness and it is through this that we can know ourselves. Beginning the process of seeing ourselves, just as we are, is the first stage of the spiritual journey.

In this stage we ask the fundamental questions, 'Who am I?' 'Where am I now?' 'What am I carrying?' and 'What am I learning?' We also look at revealing the self, identify models of experience and see how we create a sense of 'I'. These questions strengthen the self in the process of transformation. We begin our spiritual journey by directing our gaze inwards to develop our consciousness of the self.

• WHO AM I? •

The first question is, 'Who am I?' You must answer this question honestly, and go on doing so, in order to provide a solid foundation for your search. You have to commit to a life practice of seeing yourself as you are behind all of your changes.

From the *Bhagavad Gita* to modern self-help books, the literature concerning the spiritual journey refers to 'self' in two different ways. The self with a small 's' refers to the small, separate, egoic self that is confined by the limitations of personality, character and conditioning – all of the rigid patterning of our lives. Whereas the Self – with a big 'S' – is known variously as Consciousness, God, God self, Higher Self, essence, core, essential self, true nature, Buddha Nature, Atman and so on.

Our small self separates everything into pairs and establishes a distinct and independent identity. The small self relates exclusively to opposites and its identity is always one-sided. All the qualities we identify with have dynamic polarities, which we project onto others. So, for example, if we consider ourselves kind, we see cruelty in someone else; if we consider ourselves generous, we see meanness in someone else and if we consider ourselves ugly, we see beauty in someone else. We project these disowned aspects of our character onto all our external relationships. Therefore, it is impossible to avoid what we do not like in ourselves. To gain awareness, understanding and insight into these projected polarities, inner work is necessary. Without inner work we just keep repeating our character dynamics, which pervade our perceptions and interactions.

We live in an age of multiplicity, where each of us is required to perform a variety of roles. Spontaneity and true responsiveness lie obscured behind a mask. Our mask is our self-image or personality: how we see and project ourselves. It is not who we really are, but how we condition ourselves to appear. When our self-image brings us happiness, success and satisfaction, we tend to be too preoccupied to explore beneath the surface. When our self-image has broken down through loss, pain or trauma, we are more liable to explore. Irina Tweedie remarked:

> When a human being is standing with both feet firmly on the ground, with both legs on the earth, he is 'quite normal'... spiritual life is very difficult, perhaps impossible. But if something is not quite right with the mind, a little wheel not working properly in the clockwork of the mind, then spiritual life is easy.[1]

As long as we identify with our created self-image, our inner and outer lives are in continual disharmony. We have come to accept this abandonment of our integrity and wholeness but surely we underestimate our loss.

Four [American Indian] elders sat at a kitchen table in an adobe building on four chairs... The youngest was sixty-five years old, the eldest over a hundred. There was something absolutely connected about the whole quality of their presence... They told me about difficulties they had been having with white people. One of their braves had recently become involved in an auto accident with a truck from the Bureau of Indian Affairs. The BIA truck had been at fault, but the BIA found a liquor bottle nearby and claimed the brave had been drinking.

'We called the young man in and we asked him if he had been drinking', one of them told me. He said, 'No'. And then this elder looked at me very directly and very simply and said, 'And he speaks truth'.

A chill went through me at that moment. It wasn't just that I believed him or that any doubt or suspicion I might have had was immediately silenced. I experienced a kind of primordial memory of a time when you just spoke truth, a time when relationships were built on trust. That's the way it was done, because that's just how people were.[2]

However much our prevailing culture cheapens authenticity, the human spirit still strives for fulfilment. However far we stray from the milieu of truth, the truth still lives within us.

Through fear and denial, many people are disconnected from true experience and feeling. Without acceptance and allowing, feelings become concealed. They develop in the unconscious, in the shadow of awareness; they grow and transform out of all recognition. We build walls of fear and denial against authenticity until we are unaware of how we truly feel.

She entered the therapy room with a smile and seated herself confidently, hurriedly informing me of how 'fine' she was. She nervously asked, 'And how are you?' and began to summarize her week enthusiastically. The rhythm of her speech was accelerating. My attention veered away from her words to what her body was conveying to me. Her eyes were wide and staring, her shoulders hunched and frozen. She looked stiff and set, like her behaviour, and I had a sensation in the pit of my stomach like excitement... like butterflies... reminding me of terror... fear! 'What is the fear about?' I asked. She looked shocked.

By refusing to collude with falseness, we support and encourage authenticity in others and ourselves. By not responding to the masks of others, we become open to true experience and genuine encounter.

'Who am I?' is the question that becomes the source for all of our questions. Answered with honesty, it is the path back to our real self.

· WHERE AM I NOW? ·

The second question is, 'Where am I now?' You must know where your life has led you. To find out where you truly are you need to look behind your mask with total honesty. The path of truth begins with your one true step. When you open, simply and honestly, to what is happening in your life, you will find yourself on solid ground.

> I woke up to myself. I saw that I had been living a fantasy-fuelled life. I had always liked stories and as a child I was always reading. It was my escape; the world left me alone when my nose was in a book. But as I grew up the edges of life and fantasy began to blur. I fantasized about who I was and I didn't want to show anyone my real self. I experienced other people through a veil of idealism. I thrived on my imagination and I imagined I was much greater than I was. One day a friend whose insight I respected said to me, 'Your fantasy world gives you fantasy rewards'. I thought, 'I'm not happy with this anymore. It doesn't fulfil me'. I woke up to myself and I decided to change.

In order to change we must turn inwards. We should become aware of our preferences and judgements: what we like and what we do not like about others and ourselves. Unacceptable personal truths become the material of the unconscious, a storehouse of the aspects of the self, which we do not want – or are unable – to acknowledge. The unconscious appears to us in dreams, imagination and projections onto other people, places and things. Out of this sorting of reality into conscious and unconscious we create a world far removed from our true self.

Our true nature is like a jewel that has been buried under earth and rock. To retrieve the jewel we must remove that which covers it. If we have been travel-

ling along a path that has taken us further away from our true nature, we ¹
be strong enough to admit it. Having admitted it, we can then do something
about it. We need to bring back to life everything we have buried within us, for
the sake of our wholeness.

Our small self clings to identity, material achievement and prestige. When
these things eclipse the light of truth within us, we need to loosen our attachment to them. There is no better story to illustrate this than the classic Zen
tale of the university professor who went to Zen Master Nan-in and said, 'I
want to learn the spiritual path'. He already had degrees and accolades and was
a leading figure in the academic world. Now he had decided to add Zen to his
list of achievements.

> The Master had tea served and a monk took the teapot to the guest. He poured
> the tea into the cup and when it was full the master said, 'More, pour more!'
> and it began to overflow and he said sternly, 'More, pour more!'.
>
> The professor, sitting with the tea flowing over his lap, finally said, 'But it
> is full, it's full Master, it's full!'.
>
> Nan-in said quietly, 'Like this cup you are full of your own opinions and
> speculations. How can I teach you unless you first empty your cup?' [3]

'Emptying your cup' is taking away what is not needed and clearing space to
make room for the unknown in our lives. It is facing our falseness, our ugliness and our helplessness. It is opening and becoming available to life.

· WHAT AM I CARRYING? ·

The third question is, 'What am I carrying?' You must consider what you need
and what you do not need for the spiritual journey. One of the ways to do this
is to look at your life and see what is important to you – who you spend your
time with, what you spend your time doing, what you value, what you honour.
Ask yourself if your answers to these questions fulfil your deepest self. Is this
how you would like your life to be? Ask yourself, 'What am I carrying? What
do I need for the journey? What do I need to shed?' The poet Brian Patten
poignantly describes the predicament:

> I packed a suitcase
> I put dust in it
> And then more dust
> I packed bits and pieces
> Of what was still living.
> I packed a suitcase
> A heart howled inside it
> A face stared up from it
> Its tongue wagging in the dust.
> With each passing second
> The complaints it made
> Seemed more obsolete
> I packed a suitcase full of dust...[4]

We may need to shed 'the dust': dependencies, excuses, playing 'victim', blame, guilt, anger, anxiety, worry and attachment. To find out what we must discard we need to develop an intimate relationship with ourselves. Our relationship with ourself is the primary one, because out of it all of our other relationships are created. We cannot have clear relationships with others – our partners, our families, our friends – without being clear about our relationship with ourself. Whatever is not acknowledged and resolved – anything short of love of ourselves – will manifest in our outer relationships. Seeing ourselves as we are shines a clear light onto all our relationships, but any obstruction casts a long shadow.

To see ourselves, we must develop self-intimacy through inner work. Meditation, writing or dialoguing, dream work, group work and personal therapy are all powerful means of exploring the self. We must uncover the history of our previous conditioning to find what has created the rigid patterning of our lives, the hooks upon which we hang our identity.

Everything that reinforces us in our isolation, constrains us within our small selves and maintains our resistance to letting go is the known. A little cartoon I once saw showed two people squashed into the first frame. One says to the other, 'I don't know if there's anything out there'. In the next frame the other replies, 'Well, how will we know if we don't look and see?' and he pokes a finger through the frame. In the next frame they both panic and cover the hole up. In the final frame you see a little box in the middle of a beautiful meadow.

There is a tiny hole in the box. The beautiful meadow is surrounded by lush vegetation, undulating hills and beyond that is a magnificent panorama.

We maintain our fear of the unknown at the high price of limiting our consciousness. The known feels all encompassing and safe although it may not be at all. We become submerged beneath our attachment to the known and our fear of the unknown. With our true nature stifled we become full of blame, shame and guilt, which become our burdens.

• WHAT AM I LEARNING? •

The fourth question is, 'What am I learning?' Your life is a series of lessons that guide you in your spiritual unfolding. When you ask yourself, 'What am I learning? What lesson am I being given?' you will notice that the same lesson arises in a variety of circumstances at any one time. The Higher Self is a patient teacher who keeps offering the lesson, in one guise or another, until you have learnt it. The patient offering of the lesson needs to be matched by your enthusiasm to learn it.

We often learn our life lessons through adverse conditions, which we must transcend to realize something new in our lives. For example, you may be thwarted, frustrated and unfulfilled as a means of transcending selfishness and learning to be generous. Or, you may suffer rejection, apathy or anonymity as a way to work through self-importance and realize humility and your intrinsic worth.

Sometimes we feel that we are never going to understand our lesson and we become despondent and frustrated. We may feel the effects of the unlearnt lesson before understanding what the lesson is and that can be particularly confusing. Nevertheless, as we persist in learning our life lessons our resistance lessens and we pass on to the next lesson almost imperceptibly. The poet Rilke wrote:

> Be patient toward all that is unsolved in your heart and try to love the questions themselves like locked rooms or books that are written in a foreign tongue. The point is to live everything. Live the questions now. Perhaps you will then gradually, without noticing it, live your way some distant day into the answers.[5]

We must learn to take seriously the lessons that life offers us, never give up in our efforts to learn from them and always strive to grasp what life is teaching us. Often we need to find a way to de-charge our emotional resistance so that we can deepen into the lesson. For example, a friend of mine was weakened by habitual resentment as a result of his experience of deep, continual abandonment at work, in his marriage and in his early childhood. His resentment was obscuring his life lesson at that time. What he needed to learn was that he was a worthy human being in spite of being abandoned. The lesson got through to him once he recognized and dealt with his resentment.

• REVEALING YOUR SELF •

Holding on to personal secrets, which are forbidden or 'bad' is a way of the self remaining separate and isolated from others. It is a way of developing a strong and defensive ego. Forbidden secrets are aspects of ourselves about which we have learnt to feel guilty and ashamed. When we find it impossible to distinguish ourselves from our issues, we need to depersonalize feelings and patterns. We make everything very personal and it is not. Feelings, patterns and behaviour are moulded by our ancestry and our environment. They emerge out of the past with no traceable beginning – a stream of karma, a series of consequences. We are caught at a particular place, at a particular moment in time, in our bodies, in this incarnation attaching to our issues most possessively. By depersonalizing our feelings, issues and patterns, we create the necessary distance – just enough for us to bring awareness and healing to ourselves – to empower us to work on ourselves. The circumstances of our individual lives are only a brief interlude in a stream of cosmic consequences. Distance from the personal dynamics of our small self reduces the 'stickiness' of guilt and self-blame that permeates our life patterns.

Sharing the experience of ourself with others is a powerful way to cut through the mask and reveal the true self. The simple act of sharing experiences can be healing and transformative, not only for us, but also for the listener. Many times I have experienced and witnessed the relief and mutual intimacy that come from the sharing of a forbidden experience, a long-held secret, an unspoken thought or illicit desire, and the glow of recognition as the listener recognizes a common experience. Alienation and isolation dissolve in the exclamation, 'I feel just like that!' or 'I have had that experience too!'. It is wonderfully liberating when we are willing to be vulnerable and release something from our store of personal secrets with which others can identify. We can give that experience to someone else – as well as to ourselves – simply by talking openly and honestly instead of holding on.

· IDENTIFYING YOUR MODELS ·

The next step is to identify the models we have created to explain how things are: how we compartmentalize the world and hide from true experience.

One of the aspects that initially attracted me to inner work was encountering people I could not fit into my existing models. When they did something that did not fit the box I had put them in, I put them in a different box. As I began to run out of boxes, I became bewildered. I would look at those people for whom I had no prepared box and think, 'What are you? Which of my models do you belong to?' They were outside of my frame of reference. I met men who could love, which challenged my models enormously; self-empowered people who could be strong and vulnerable, when these two qualities were mutually exclusive according to my models, and people who could be angry or needy without guilt. I began to aspire to these new models because I wanted them in my life.

I encourage you to develop new models, either from people who challenge your boxes or from imagining how you would like things to be. Free yourself from the limitations of your old models – your father, your mother, your brother, your sister or your schoolteacher – and break out of your rigid pattern of separateness and isolation.

A couple that I know live on a mountaintop in Southern Spain. They are living their lives true to their beliefs and in line with their hearts. Yet they told me that fifteen years ago they were entrenched in the 'rat race'. She worried about wearing the 'right' clothes and meeting the 'right' people. He was driven to work for high pay in a job which clashed with his principles.

After years of living what they now call 'a hollow existence' they decided to quit their high-powered and financially rewarding jobs to travel to different countries. They saw many different ways of living and models of happiness and their experiences provided the turnaround they both desired. They did not return to their jobs, but continued to pursue their vision of a more wholesome and rewarding life, which was more authentic for them.

•SPIRITUAL AND HUMAN•

It is through the heart that you understand the reality of the self and its relationship to the Higher Self. Your heart is the bridge between your humanness and your divinity; for each is an aspect of your wholeness. Following a spiritual path in the world requires learning to flow between the small, separate self and the Higher Self. You do not have to deny the individual self.

The most spiritual people are the most human people because spirituality is the flowering of full humanity. There is no essential difference between spirituality and humanity. When you are in your personality and everything that goes with it, *be there*. It is not separate from the Self. Allow your personality to be informed by your consciousness and develop your individuality with awareness unbounded by limiting or negative models.

•THE IMAGINARY 'I'•

Seeing ourselves as we are poses the question, 'What are the differences between how I really am and my self-image?' The answers demand total honesty and nothing less. This question underlies all of the subsequent stages of the journey. We have to return to it repeatedly to see through illusion. The imaginary 'I' is a momentary creation of our minds. Stephen Levine remarks:

> When choosing who we wish we were, we cull from the great mix an image here and there, and discredit the rest through some rationalization. What we choose, or what is allowed to remain, we call 'I' – believing all the while that this 'I' is choosing rather than what has actually been chosen.[6]

We create the 'I' then identify it as our real self – but who created the 'I' in the first place?

Seeing ourselves as we are can be like finding the end of a ball of string. The question, 'Who am I?' can lead us to our intuitive, wise heart. We have to face up to our ugliness and helplessness, our beauty and empowerment, our inner binds and contradictions and surpass self-deception and ignorance. Although our nature is human and divine – and the two are not truly distinct from each other – we must begin the journey by clearly distinguishing the small, separate self from the true Self. We must separate to join. The spiritual path is the way of balance, wholeness and unity.

A man came and knocked at a friend's door: his friend asked him, 'Who art thou?' He answered, 'I'.

The friend said, 'Be gone, there's no room here'. The man went away and spent a year in travel and in separation from his friend until he realized his error and returned to the door and knocked again.

His friend called to him, 'Who is at the door'. 'Thou', answered the man. 'Now', said the friend, 'since thou art I' come in. There is not room in the house for two 'I's'.

Every moment brings an opportunity for seeing 'I' in 'Thou', 'Thou' in 'I' and for seeing ourselves as we really are.

DEVELOPING FAITH

The stupid man looks at his body and says, 'This is I'. The more learned thinks, 'This is I' of his personality. But the wise man knows the true Self, saying, 'I am the Eternal'. He is individual, though without separateness. He who possesses Soul vision has dissolved the 'I' in Pure Consciousness.

Shankara

And therefore saith Saint Paul of himself and many others thus: Although our bodies be presently here on earth, nevertheless our living is in heaven.

The Cloud of Unknowing

We are immersed in our experience of the body and the five senses, and identified exclusively with our personality, which is a perpetual creation of our mind. We define ourselves within the limitations of the body and the personality. But if we seek to define ourselves by these two aspects of the self only, then we must deny the spiritual Self.

We are consciousness, which is not bound by natural laws, since it is eternal. We are not our bodies and our senses, because our bodies die. We are not our minds or our personalities, because we ourselves are the creators of both. Within the limitations of body and mind we may have spiritual experience, but we can never realize our spiritual essence. On the spiritual journey we need to develop faith in order to transcend the world of mind and body.

In this stage we look at how the Divine reveals itself, faith and desire, the body and the five senses, personality and consciousness, and the lessons of life. The essence of this stage is 'going beyond,' without certainty; but with faith.

·HOW THE DIVINE SHOWS ITSELF: FOOTPRINTS AND FAITH·

The intuitive knowledge of the world of the spirit comes in many ways – the memory of a 'glow' in childhood, an indescribable impression in the heart, an experience of 'otherness'. It can come through scriptures, direct experience, or deep insight.

In an image from *Kakuan's Ten Bulls* – a series of Zen Buddhist pictures from the twelfth century that depict the search for our true nature[1] – the herdsman, who symbolizes the small self, sees footprints, the mark of the bull, which represents his true nature. On the evidence of the footprints he begins his search. He has not yet seen the bull, so he cannot be certain of its existence, but the footprints are enough for him to start looking. He acts out of faith.

Intuiting the bull from the footprints is like sensing the Divine from its effects. What do the footprints mean to you? Have you seen the marks of your true nature in your own life? Whatever way the Divine has manifested in our lives, it leaves us with the certainty of peace, love and eternity 'which passeth all understanding' – it points to a reality beyond the material world.

In the *Bhagavad Gita*, Krishna says:

> From the world of the senses comes heat and comes cold, and pleasure and pain. They come and they go: they are transient. Arise above them, strong soul.[2]

The world of the senses is relative; the meeting with the Divine is absolute. The five senses connect us to the world of soul and nature, 'grounding' our spirits. The Divine is ever-present but to experience It fully – and not just see 'the footprints' – all our senses must be, as St. John of the Cross wrote, 'in bliss suspended'.[3]

We are always surrounded by this bliss. The ancient *Vedas* – the oldest sacred texts of India – spoke of *turiya*, the fourth state, the state of enlightenment. The first three states of waking, sleeping and dreaming describe the human condition. *Turiya* permeates and witnesses these other states, eternally existing and transcending duality.[4]

> We are the mirror as well as the face in it.
> We are tasting the taste this minute
> Of eternity. We are pain
> And what cures pain. We are
> The sweet cold water and the jar that pours.[5]

·Faith and Desire·

Rising above the senses leads to the understanding that desire is empty, because desire is always trying to fill what we presume to be lack in us. Swami Vivekananda noted:

> Desire is infinite, its fulfilment limited. Desire is unlimited in everyone.[6]

Ultimately, satisfaction is the absence of desire, so that no amount of action motivated by desire will ever bring true satisfaction. When we comprehend the emptiness of desire, reflected back to us in our belief of a never-ending lack; the helplessness and despair may be overwhelming.

Alternatively, the emptiness of desire may fuel our spiritual search. The five senses connect us to the sensual world, the soul and desire; they do not unite us with the Divine. They may take us as far as 'the footprints' but we will not reach God by way of the senses. To arrive there you have to transcend them.

This stage calls for our faith and trust: faith in the unknown and trust in the process of life. Following our intuition of something beyond the body and the five senses, beyond mind and personality, is the true beginning of spiritual seeking. Faith may be all we have at this stage. We may sometimes be persuaded to look ahead, but when we do we find an absence of faith, because faith always lives in the present moment, never in the future. We need to strengthen the self to serve the Divine as in the *Vedic* saying, 'The harder the wood, the brighter the flame, when it burns in the fire of the spirit'.

If you have friends who are entirely bound by mind and body, they will find spiritual faith incomprehensible. Find kindred spirits who are committed to their own spiritual path. Spiritual isolation can put you, unnecessarily, in a precarious and vulnerable situation. A group, a *sangha*, a community of like-minded people offers valuable support to the followers of the spiritual path. Best of all is the discovery of those around you who turn out to be kindred spirits and form your deep community. Usually they are much closer than you would ever suspect.

When you are isolated on the spiritual path, you can become disillusioned and misdirected. It requires exceptional inner strength to follow your deep truth with no support.

Once there lived a village of creatures along the bottom of a great crystal river. The current of the river swept silently over them all – young and old, rich and poor, good and evil, the current going its own way, knowing only its own crystal self. Each creature in its own manner clung tightly to the twigs and rocks of the river bottom, for clinging was their way of life, and resisting the current what each had learned from birth. But one creature said at last, 'I am tired of clinging. Though I cannot see it with my eyes, I trust that the current knows where it is going. I shall let go and let it take me where it will. Clinging, I shall die of boredom'. The other creatures laughed and said, 'Fool! Let go and that current you worship will throw you tumbled and smashed across the rocks and you will die quicker than boredom!'. But the one heeded them not and taking a breath did let go and at once was tumbled and smashed by the current across the rocks. Yet in time, as the creature refused to cling again, the current lifted him free from the bottom, and he was bruised and hurt no more. And the creatures downstream to whom he was a stranger cried, 'See a miracle! A creature like ourselves, yet he flies! See the Messiah come to save us all!' And the one carried in the current said, 'I am no more Messiah than you. The river delights to lift us free, if only we dare let go. Our true work is this voyage, this adventure'.[7]

The world is benign: it responds to our trust and it supports us in our journey. The world feeds and nourishes us – when we allow it to. And when we learn to have faith in life we can savour the journey.

·THE BODY AND THE FIVE SENSES·

The body and the five senses have a dual nature. We taste, smell, hear, touch and see – walking barefoot on dew-drenched grass, listening to Mozart or the rhythmic strum of a guitar, smelling the scent of freshly-picked coriander or lavender, tasting ripe fruit or a dish flavoured with exotic spices, hearing and speaking with voices which touch the heart and set the pulse racing with excitement and inspiration, watching a beautiful sunset – through the body. Conversely, we endure the pain of injury, illness and disease, hear screams and cruel words, smell decay and noxious stenches, taste sour milk, sense extreme physical discomfort or nausea and take in images of ugliness and horror – also through the body. The body and its senses both attract and repel.

The body binds us to the material world, of which it is a part, but we are matter filled with and vivified by spirit. The body is the creation of our consciousness; it is the form of our soul and the shape of our spirit. Our relationship to the material world mirrors our identification with the body, as our relationship to our bodies reflects our identification with the material world.

I had decided to take some time off. I had become physically exhausted, psychologically jaded and full of questions. I needed some time for myself to balance and heal, as well as a radical rethink about my life. I sold my house, loaded all my belongings into a van and drove down to a storage warehouse. When everything was stacked in, I stood back and looked at this powerful cube of objects which contained all the material acquisitions of my life. I wanted to rejoice wholeheartedly in the freedom of having little more than what I could hold and enough money to travel wherever I wanted to. But the cube of objects exerted a subtle pull on me. My spirit was attached to them by an invisible umbilical cord. As I gazed at the things – furniture, television, computer, sound system, clothes, rugs, kitchen utensils, pictures – I realized that they reflected my body and senses and that, without a body, I wouldn't need any of these things. My whole self, my historical self, was here in the photo albums, old letters, documents and souvenirs – all of me was here in this cube! It seemed so obvious I couldn't believe I hadn't seen it before: I had created all of this stuff – from my house to my wash-bag to the loose change in my pocket – out of my dependence and attachment to my body!

• PERSONALITY AND YOUR STORY •

Personality is simply the 'packaging' which creates your superficial identity. It cushions and protects you as you meet the world. Personality is created and supported by a finely honed story, which is original and unique.

Your personal story does not describe who you are, only what you have become. Underneath you may fear that there is nothing real and this is because you are out of touch with your true nature.

When we sleep we place the small self on standby. We revive it in the morning. Usually before we even open our eyes, we begin recreating ourselves. This is a powerful addiction. Our personality forms false relationships that suit our personal stories. This is always a barrier to true intimacy because the personality is only a mask. When we are willing to drop the mask and reveal ourselves without reserve, true intimacy can take place. While our masks are in place our relationships are superficial – a dance of appearance and projection. We contract, separate, create the drama of our lives, and maintain the delusion of connectedness.

Personality fixes and confines us. We construct our personality from a complex and convoluted account of the events of our lives. We fix this account in memory and repeat it endlessly, which both trivializes and strengthens it. Telling our story turns into an empty ritual that honours the past and obscures the real experience. We cling to the description and the sequence of our stories.

With no personal story, the self would not exist. Regard your personality lightly, like a thin coat that keeps the rain off. Carry your personality and your story easily and comfortably, without clinging too tightly. Let personality serve you in the world of appearances, but be aware that there is more to you.

The perception of 'I' is associated with a form, which may be the body. There should be nothing associated with the pure Self. The Self is the unassociated, pure reality, in whose light the body and the ego shine. On stilling all thoughts the pure consciousness remains.

Ramana Maharshi

What do you see when you glimpse someone with a usually strong personality in an unguarded moment? Often they are quite unrecognizable because you see the real person beneath the mask. Personality should be seen through, even discarded, when appropriate. For example, if you are sitting alone on a mountain top, or sharing an intimate moment with a loved one, what use is your personality?

Work with your personality, get to know it and then slowly loosen your tight hold and your dependency on it. Personality perpetuates the rigid pattern of your small self. Personality is limiting, separating and contracting. Give attention to your personal story: let it emerge, write it down and reflect on it. What does your personality conceal? What are you afraid of? How could you let down the mask of personality and reveal your deeper self?

· CONSCIOUSNESS AND FORM ·

In the Buddhist *Scripture of Great Wisdom* there is a stark and forthright expression of the relationship between form and the formless:

Void is all form... for what is form is void.[8]

Far from being a philosophy of nihilism, which this may at first seem, this insight can lead you to your true nature. You are consciousness in form and consciousness is empty, void and formless. Out of such profound emptiness everything comes into being. The challenge of being human and divine is seeing the emptiness in appearance and the appearance in emptiness. We should learn to see things as they are: to see the transcendent in the ordinary and the ordinary in the transcendent. The void is the matrix of creation, the chalice that contains the mysterious, inexhaustible, life-giving waters. The sage Lao Tzu tells us:

The spirit of the valley never dies.
This is called the mysterious female.
The gateway of the mysterious female
Is called the root of heaven and earth.
Dimly visible, it seems as if it were there,
Yet use will never drain it.[9]

The body and its senses are our physical form and our personality is our mental form. But the Higher Self is beyond form: we will never discover it in our physical body or our intellect. We are not our form. We mistake the dying candle for the shining light. Our appearance is the light play of God, as the moon's appearance is the reflection of the sun's rays. Our body, the five senses, our minds and the creations of our minds – including the personality – are mere fleeting creations. Truth, the reality we seek, is beyond the passing creation of form. Roshi Jiyu Kennett wrote:

...the photograph of my dead mother is but an empty imprint on paper of that which is already something else; if I place it in the fire that which was paper will immediately become ashes – where is there any photograph, where my mother? – both took form, became void and took form again.[10]

Spiritually, the construction of personality, image and appearance is of no consequence. Consciousness is void and beyond form. When we understand that the mind creates 'substance', which is ultimately insubstantial, and that form and the void are the same then we are liberated from illusion.

Your divinity is in your humanity as your humanity is in your divinity. Your freedom is to be found in your restriction; your spiritual liberation through your human limitation. The meeting of pairs of opposites, in fulfilment of wholeness and unity, teaches us that life is a circle, with no beginning and no end.

The realization that you are neither your personality, nor your body, leads to the intuitive understanding that everything is an expression of the Divine, that all form is a manifestation of the Self. You have completed a single revolution of the circle and now the forms of the small separate self can be re-visioned as divine, *in themselves*. The self is the Self. As long as we have developed this insight, and made it our own, we need no longer distinguish between them.

·INNOCENCE AND SIMPLICITY·

The path of innocence is smoother than the path of doubt. While doubt guards, resists, distrusts, hesitates and obstructs, innocence allows, opens, trusts and follows. Innocence is a wise virtue and an ally of faith. Whether we follow innocence or doubt will depend on our personalities. But the path of innocence is responsive, open, straightforward, transparent and simple. Our vulnerability becomes a strength and we learn quickly. Of course there are disadvantages – we can be fooled for example – but we can learn from all of our experiences. When we weigh up innocence against doubt, innocence is the wiser choice.

Unless our early life has been unusual, education, family life and upbringing will have each contributed to a deep denial of our innocence. Imagination and daydreaming, as well as innocence, are systematically denied in our culture. Examples of original innocents fulfilling their destinies are found in such diverse sources as myth (Parsifal in the legend of the Holy Grail), folk tales (Vasalisa the Wise), divination (The Fool in the tarot), and, by derivation, modern movies (from Peter Sellers in *Being There* to Tom Hanks in *Forest Gump*).

Simplicity is another wise virtue. The ability to find fulfilment in each moment without striving for more and the capacity to reflect and inhabit a rich inner world are qualities that can keep us positive and buoyant even when we are surrounded by complexity, confusion and opposition. We tend to feel that adverse conditions will last forever. This feeling exacerbates our situation and we may lose hope of a respite, even though change is inevitable. Like innocence, simplicity is a quality of our essence, of our true nature. As we journey on the spiritual path our essence is gradually realized.

Simplicity takes each moment as it comes and does not multiply its intensity by projecting into the future. Thich Nhat Hanh writes:

> As you let go of worry and sorrow, bring a smile to your face. This may be just a beginning of a smile, but keep it on your lips, like the Buddha's half-smile. Learn to walk as a Buddha walks, to smile as a Buddha smiles. This half-smile is the fruit of awareness and joyful peace of mind, and it also nurtures and preserves that awareness and peaceful joy. It is truly miraculous.[11]

·IDENTITY AND FEAR·

A story is told of a god who was united in undifferentiated eternal consciousness. And it thought, 'I am'. Immediately it was afraid because it was now a being born in time. It thought, 'But I have nothing to be afraid of, I am the only thing there is'. Immediately it felt lonely and yearned for another and so, for the first time, it felt desire.

Our first experience of fear comes with the rhythmic contraction of the uterus. In our purely natural state in the womb there is no sense of 'I'. From where then does this sense of 'I' come? The self should be understood, or re-visioned, so we see *what it is not*. This is the task of the second stage and it is vital to the journey. This is our opportunity to strip ourselves of the fundamental illusion of selfhood – to go beyond the visible, egoic, separative 'I am' out of which fear and desire arise.

In this stage we can find ourselves in a precarious, 'in-between' position. The common sense world of personality, the body and the five senses is insufficient to realize the Divine, but we have not yet arrived at a place beyond common sense. We become vulnerable to fear; but strong in faith. We cannot explain, justify or argue for our faith, and remain faithful to ourselves; we cannot rationalize and remain true to our vision. We are doing the necessary work of strengthening the self through uncertainty.

Uncertainty is one of the challenges that prepares us for the work of spiritual transformation, which asks nothing less than everything. Like many aspects of the spiritual journey, the very process we are in is spiritually instructive in itself. We are being taught how to live in the Self and our teacher is Life.

· THE LESSONS OF SUFFERING ·

'How are you living your life now?' Answer this question and you will find out everything you need to know at this stage. Most of us are imbalanced, leaning away from our centres precariously, yet never expecting to fall. Our true nature seeks balance and both body and mind, if allowed to 'be', reflect this tendency. We become 'being' through a process of simplification. Through watching the thoughts and actions that our attractions and aversions provoke in us, we become aware of our motivations and intentions. As we try to simplify ourselves, stillness deepens within us and this stillness grows from the profound acceptance of the present circumstances of our lives.

Buddha said that life is suffering and that the primary cause of suffering is delusion. We are deluded by our senses and, in Buddhism, there is a sixth sense, which is the intellect. The six senses cause us to regard the world of changing appearances as ultimate reality. The divine illusion of diversity and change is called *maya*. The small, separate self creates *maya* out of the projection of inner conflicts. Enlightenment takes the middle route between suffering and not-suffering, light and dark, life and death, good and bad. Can you see the lesson in the 'in-between'? Our path leads between the pairs of opposites. We favour neither side but aim at balance, intending towards the middle. This is the way of less self-

We are imprisoned within the body, like an oyster within a shell. Plato

35

ness, less resistance, more allowing and more acceptance. Joseph Campbell relates this anecdote:

> I have a friend who… has a bone disease that has involved an experience of great pain throughout her life… I said to this woman, 'You've got to say 'yes' to this. This terrible pain that's with you all the time is your Guru, your teacher. This is what has honed you into the beautiful person you are, and your pain and suffering is what builds your life and your character, and somehow or other you have affirmed this from the very beginning… find where your pain is and by saying 'yes' to it, the whole new consciousness will suddenly be experienced.[12]

Pain can be your guru – or depression, migraines, thwarted ambition, intolerance, your mother, your son or a flat tyre! Your adversary turns out to be your helper. However hard the challenge is in your life, misery, torment and unrest bring the deepest transformation when you say 'yes'.

Mind and body are one; the psychological is the physical. Both mind and body are the creations of consciousness. They complement each other like heat and flame, like music and silence.

Illness is frequently the embodiment of messages from the unconscious in physical form. These messages, interpreted skilfully, can lead us to wholeness. Often an illness makes us aware of hidden aspects of ourselves and causes us to integrate them whether or not we are aware of this process.

Behind our impulse towards balance is the call of our Higher Self. Often the urging of the Higher Self is ignored when we deny our intuition, neglect our emotions, or resist opportunities for change. Intuition, emotions and change are all a risk to the small self.

We are also moved towards balance in our dealings with the world in the unfolding of our personalities and our progress through life. Losing our job, the breakdown of our relationship, public scandal, mental disturbance may all be the unconscious acting out of the hidden aspects of our lives. As the unconscious aspects of the self exert their influence, we are brought closer to our spiritual centre. When what we value is taken away from us, we experience loss, often followed by the knowledge that we were dissatisfied anyway.

Recognize your lessons. Life is always offering you teaching in the present moment, sometimes in too obvious a way for you to value. All your lessons point to something beyond the body and the personality. Identifying yourself in the temporal world as your body and your personality both causes and substantiates your fears. Lao Tzu advised:

Welcome disgrace as a pleasant surprise.
Prize calamities as your own body.
Because our body is the very source of our calamities.
If we have no body, what calamities can we have?[13]

Deep within us we sense that our body and our personality are transient things. We are absorbed in the changing cycle of life, which we can see all around us. Nothing remains the same; everything is in constant flux. Our identification with mind and body is the futile attempt of the small, separate self to fix itself in space and time. But we find ourselves in this flow of change, and fear is the inevitable outcome of trying to resist the current. We can never enter the river in the same place twice.

If we accept change with openness, practice faith in action and grow in our commitment to our spiritual journey, we move gradually past fear to embark on a journey of discovery and enlightenment.

I had been stuck in a cycle of feeling frustrated, angry and powerless. However much I vented my rage, I remained unable to release or transcend it. I developed a gangrenous appendix, which burst. The resulting peritonitis had been very hard to diagnose and, after hours of painful tests and probing, I had undergone an investigative operation, which left me with a large vertical scar down my abdomen. For over a year, I had felt extremely sensitive about the incision and the scar. I felt deeply wounded and walked 'bent' in the middle of my body. I felt like a decrepit old man even though I was only then in my late twenties. One day I was lying down with my hands folded and my fingers interlocked over the scar and, spontaneously, I found myself asking to be healed. Although my eyes were closed I 'saw' a pair of pure white wings above me, which very tenderly waved together and, as they did so, I had a 'sensation beyond sensation' of my wound being sealed by a pair of divine hands and healed. I was elated by the profundity and bliss of what had happened to me. After that I began to walk and be in my body again without feeling wounded and in pain.

· Part 2·

THE JOURNEY AROUND THE SELF

AWARENESS

We mistake the clear light of pure awareness for the shadows that it casts in consciousness. Pure awareness, pure is-ness, has no personal identification – it is the essence of being itself...
Stephen Levine

The third stage of the spiritual journey marks our commitment to the spiritual practice of raising our consciousness – to becoming aware. We are motivated to practise awareness for many different reasons: out of spiritual longing, to find understanding, to heal dissatisfaction with our lives, to emulate a teacher or a spiritual mentor. The virtue and the necessity of awareness practice are that we balance being with doing, harmonize body and spirit, and become closer to our true selves.

Awareness is an occupation like no other because, not only is it a practice, but it is also our natural condition. It is not just what we *do*; it is what we *are*. Awareness practice is the very heart of spirituality and is to be found in the deepest teachings of all the great spiritual traditions.

In this stage we face the challenge of transforming the quality of our awareness, unifying consciousness, working with the judgemental mind, developing the witness, seeing how change flows out of grace, understanding the relationship of failure and humility, dealing with unfinished business, becoming 'the knower' and cultivating clarity, healing and insight.

·Two Kinds of Awareness·

To deepen our understanding of the practice we should distinguish two kinds of awareness. First, there is spacious awareness, which is yin, female, wide and defocused. Second, there is concentrated awareness, which is yang, male, narrow and focused. Both kinds of awareness are recognizable in both ancient and modern sources.

In a four thousand year-old Tantric teaching that gives 112 ways to spiritual liberation[1] the two kinds of awareness are represented. The teaching is presented as an exchange between two deities, Shiva and his consort Devi, 'in a language of love we have yet to learn'. In answer to Devi's enquiry about the nature of reality, Shiva chants a marvellous series of meditations, each one a path to enlightenment in itself.

Contemporary instruction books on meditation reflect the same distinction. For example, we can watch a candle flame and, as we get distracted, gently bring ourselves back to the object of concentration. If we do this for forty minutes, we find that our awareness is more acute. Returning our awareness to any other object of attention achieves the same result. Moreover, we can attempt to follow our in breath and our out breath throughout the day and notice that each time we start a conversation, we forget our breath practice altogether! When we notice what has happened, we can gently bring ourselves back to breath awareness again. The candle and the breath meditations are both examples of concentrated awareness, which excludes everything but the object of awareness.

Spacious awareness, on the other hand, is all-inclusive. For example, if we bring our awareness to where we are right now – opening to the totality of the present moment, not distinguishing any single thing – and meditate on it as a unity, then we are practicing spacious awareness. Another example is making 'sound' the object of our awareness – no specific single sound, which requires focused awareness, but all-inclusive sound.

Either focused or defocused attention will bring you, through a process of inner balancing and harmony, to a deeper state of awareness.

If you have been working hard with focused awareness – for example doing a repetitive task that demands an intense, narrow focus, which many jobs require for eight hours a day – and you stop, you will drop into defocused awareness. This is because you have a tendency towards balance. Both spacious and concentrated attention are aspects of awareness. Sometimes both are needed.

When I am leading a workshop, I may find that I lose touch with the group when my all attention is drawn to a particular individual. This can happen very easily. Similarly, I may lose touch with an individual when the group takes up all my attention. I balance these two extremes by practising being flexible and responding to what is needed in the moment. When I am fluid and flowing between these two kinds of awareness, I am most present.

Spacious awareness and concentrated awareness are two different modes of relationship. Consider which is easier for you in relation to your character. Challenge yourself by extending your tolerance of the way that is harder for you. Play with these modes of awareness lightly, separately and together, allowing you to connect and relate to the world.

•AWARENESS SHOWS YOU YOURSELF•

When we begin an awareness practice we are confronted with ourselves. We notice how the runaway processes of the mind enslave us. Buddhists call this 'monkey mind'. If we have a tendency to intellectualize, awareness begins as an intellectual practice. Similarly, if we are dominated by emotions, awareness begins as an emotional practice. We should exert persistent, gentle effort to return the mind to stillness. After a while the mind becomes less restless and more settled and we feel more relaxed and peaceful. But something more happens through this discipline. We *become* the awareness we are practising and the runaway processes of the mind become the object of our awareness. This is a pivotal point of meditation.

Our internal conflicts can find external expression when we start to practise awareness. For example, we might feel peaceful and centred when we are in our place of meditation, but when we go out to work, we lose our centre and our peace and worry and struggle replaces them as we deal with the challenges of the working day. When we come home from work and sit in meditation we feel peaceful again.

The creation of a respectful space may be an aid to meditation, but awareness practice should not be restricted to peaceful environments. The object of our awareness is whatever is before us; true meditation is in each moment.

Sometimes we experience peace within and turmoil outside of us. At other times, we experience turmoil within and peace outside of us. When things are too peaceful, the mind seizes the opportunity to throw up all its turmoil, noise and confusion. Similarly, when we are practising awareness in a commotion, we may experience great calm. Each of these experiences reflects the tendency of our consciousness to balance. From this balance, we experience inner calm and peace wherever we are.

·The Clouds or the Open Sky·

Focused awareness tends to be more valued in our culture. It reflects the ethos of 'doing'– work, acquisition and achievement. It is the attitude that 'gets things done'. We learn how to criticize and compare ourselves with other people. We load our awareness with critical attention and focus on our faults, our mistakes and our deficiencies – sometimes exclusively. We suffer from intense scrutiny of our feelings and our lives. We become totally caught up with ourselves as separate identities engaged in personal dramas.

Spacious awareness can be likened to a painting canvas; the brush strokes to our personal dramas. When we can see the blank canvas behind the brush-strokes, we are practising spacious awareness. When we see the brush-strokes only, we are in concentrated awareness. When we see both – distinct yet connected – we experience the totality.

Awareness is both a practice – acting *as if* – and your true condition, how you really are. A traditional method that gives you a taste of this distinction is the meditation on the clouds and the open sky. You can focus on the clouds that are passing across the sky or you can defocus your awareness to the blue sky that is always there behind the clouds. You are both. You are the passing clouds – all which is fleeting and changeable in your life – and the endless sky – the unchangeable, the deathless in you. Your awareness chooses between the clouds and the sky in much the same way as you choose between your personality and the Divine in your life.

·Only One Consciousness·

Each of us is a part of unified Consciousness. If you and I are practising awareness, and we are looking at the clouds, we can meet and make contact of a sort. Alternatively, if we are practising awareness and are both absorbed in the sky, we are in the same place instantly. We may not choose to meet at all but, if we do, there will be a real meeting between us. If you meet someone and you are both with the clouds, then you are just a couple of people enveloped in your own problems and dramas. If you meet someone and you are both practising looking at the sky, so that you are identified with the blank canvas, then there is immediate resonance, because there is only one consciousness. At the heart of all things is the one Truth. In *Kakuan's Ten Bulls* it is expressed this way:

> This unity is like salt in water, like colour in dyestuff. The slightest thing is not apart from Self.[2]

The tendency for most of us is to focus on our lives and ourselves to the extent that we become overwhelmed by the intensity of our own self-absorption. We need to move out of this preoccupation with ego-dominated, over-focused awareness into a more expansive awareness to create balance in our lives.

To begin to experience unified Consciousness, start by denying your separation – from anyone, from anything, from the Divine itself. Deny the reality of all thoughts and ideas that are limiting – past and future, inner and outer, and so on. To discover the peace in unity, meditate on the One.

·JUDGEMENTAL MIND·

The judgemental mind is the polar opposite of the aware mind. In pure awareness, everything is as it is, completely accepted without partiality. But our minds are eager to stamp an assessment on everything we perceive. We begin watching a simple candle and before long we have calculated its shape, the rate it burns, how much it costs, and which direction the draft is coming from to cause the wax to run down one side. We assess, criticize, evaluate and spin off in endless associations and enquiries which take us far away from the candle as it is.

Judgement is the hard face of insecurity, the unforgiving face of fear, which strengthens our identity. It is very difficult for us to look at anyone or anything without judging. The comparison inherent in judgement marginalizes the other and inflates our ego. The raft of judgement, criticism and comparison rides on waves of anxiety, worthlessness and fear.

You become aware that you are not truly aware because of your judgemental mind. Slowly, through awareness practice, you notice how you criticize and assess everyone and everything in tremendous detail and you want everyone to like you – whoever they are. This creates an inner contradiction. Even as you are judging others, you are seeking their approval. You judge and criticize until everything is imperfect, and then you despair.

> You are awareness. Awareness is another name for you. Since you are awareness there is no need to attain or cultivate it. All that you have to do is to give up being aware of other things, that is of the not-Self. If one gives up being aware of them then pure awareness alone remains, and that is the Self.[3]

The practice, and state, of awareness is to open simply to *what is*. A good method is to challenge ourselves with whatever we dislike and practise non-discrimination; to simply open, without following our preference or our loathing. We have so much resistance to opening to how things are, but the more we open, the more we learn. When we are open to experience, everything teaches us. When everything is teaching us, we see the Divine in everything.

Awareness gives the mind a rest. We need to learn to be able to use our mind and not be used by it. As thoughts appear, we notice them, like passing clouds, and return gently to awareness. Always be gentle with yourself; never be harsh or critical; these qualities only create resistance in you.

•AWARENESS, ACCEPTANCE, CHANGE•

A little philosophy which has come out of my observation and understanding of working with people can be summed up in three words – awareness, acceptance, change. This process is very powerful. Awareness creates acceptance and acceptance leads to change. There is a fourth element and that is grace or divine influence.

We can change through a simple awareness practice. When we intend to be present in each moment, to be with diverse conditions without judging, to be a witness to the self, we gradually create and nurture a deep inner acceptance. As this acceptance deepens, we enter a state of grace. This is a deep surrender to life and the mystery of existence. When this happens we may experience a feeling of suspension, a tantalizing delay, an 'inhalation' in time. We become restless and dissatisfied. Staying with this stage demands a great tolerance of inaction and an acceptance of profound waiting. The pregnant suspension reaches a point of profound stillness and – following a little delay – change occurs.

This process is central to my therapy practice. Simply by being together and sharing thoughts and feelings, everything becomes more vivid. It is like adjusting the focus on a camera. As we fine-tune our awareness, we become deeply present. We rest in life as it is, in perfect acceptance of the moment. We become witnesses to change as we notice the moment flowing away from us and arrive at a deep acceptance. Whether this process takes weeks, months or years; we are never the same again.

Change is a mystery because it is entirely outside your control. When something really changes, it is lovely to see. It is like a wave breaking. We cannot make the wave break sooner. If you have ever been out on a surfboard or playing in the waves at the beach, you will know the deliciousness and excitement of anticipating the moment when the wave will break. Maybe the wave will surprise you and come sooner than you think or maybe it will take longer. There is nothing you can do; you are powerless to affect it either way. What will happen depends on the moon, the tides and the forces of nature. When the wave will occur is uncertain; that there will be a wave, however, is a certainty. It is like this with grace-given change, which comes in its own time with no concern for our impatience or desire.

· FAILURE AND HUMILITY ·

Awareness is a humbling practice because mostly we learn through our failures. We try to fail less each time, but often the more we try to be aware the less aware we are. Awareness should be effortless and unselfconscious. It should be practiced so naturally that we forget about awareness altogether. In fact, we would only truly be aware if we were unaware that we were aware!

The Russian philosopher and mystic PD Ouspensky provided many frustrating examples of the elusiveness of practising awareness.[4] For example, he suggests you follow a watch-hand around a circular watch-face and remain aware only of the watch-hand – but you cannot do it. The watch ticks once, twice and already you have become distracted.

But the failure produces a curious and essential by-product, and that is humility. No aspect of the practice of awareness can be used for the glorification of the small, separate self. Just to engage in awareness is humbling and an expression of the very thing we seek – the dissolving of our separateness into the Self.

· Unfinished Business and Loose Ends ·

We create unfinished business whenever we leave loose ends in our lives. Whether we are aware of it or not, our unfinished business always has our energy attached to it. In some cases, all that is necessary is to 'go back' and sort things out. In other cases, it might be more significant and crucial to get our energy back first and see what has to be sorted out afterwards.

We have become attached to the idea of sorting things out first, but we can do it the other way round. We do not have to wait to get our energy back. There comes a time when we realize that no one is losing out, except ourselves, so why wait any longer? RD Laing said, 'The prison door's open, why are you still in the prison?'[5] We do not have to do the work first; we can get out now. Nothing need prevent our escape from our personal prison. Later, if necessary, we can work with our tendency to get caught in patterns that try to tempt us back in.

Find the courage to deal with your unfinished business. Start in small ways. Each day, each hour you do not have to leave things unsaid or unfinished. Finishing unfinished business is good practice and it is vital for practising awareness. Unfinished business recurs until you deal with it. So work with unresolved situations and relationships and reclaim any parts of yourself that you have left with other people and situations.

· The Part of You that Knows ·

In each of us there is a part that knows. We are all familiar with the part that does not know, but we know much more than we are willing to admit. To live what we know, we have to cross the borders of the small, separate self.

I used to see a therapist who would ask me something about myself and when I said, 'I don't know', he would say, 'What about the part of you that does know?' I felt irritated and confused. I thought, 'Why does he keep asking me this?' But the question began to get through to me. What was I getting angry about? I started to see I had these two doors inside. I had an old door marked, 'I don't know', and another that my therapist insisted was there. No one had ever told me about that door before. Finding it was very liberating because it moved back the self-imposed limitations of my inner world and opened up new possibilities and a deeper responsibility to life. Anthony de Mello wrote:

> There's nothing so delightful as being aware. Would you rather live in darkness? Would you rather act and not be aware of your actions, talk and not be aware of your words? Would you rather listen to people and not be aware of what you're hearing, or see things and not be aware of what you're looking at?[6]

When you find out that you know, your life changes. You are able to face up to things honestly, take responsibility, and be decisive. You do not let yourself get away with things like you used to, because the 'knower' in you is present. No excuses! Immediacy, knowing what you want and what you need, replaces your unfinished business, clears the next hurdle and prevents you putting things off.

Every time you hear that voice saying, 'I don't know,' ask, 'What about the part of me that does know?' It is the part you refer to for help and for guidance, that tells you what you need to know and what you need to do. It might come as an intuition, a hunch, a visual picture, or a feeling. It is always there for you and whenever you think you do not know, that is where your fear is and that is the edge for you to work at. If you are unclear about any area of yourself, then take yourself to the door of your knowing and ask. Do not let fear prevent you from doing that.

Swami Vivekananda wrote:

> ... all knowledge comes from the human soul. Man manifests knowledge, discovers it within himself, which is pre-existing through eternity. Everyone is the embodiment of Knowledge...[7]

Deep inner knowing comes from the heart, knowledge from the mind. DT Suzuki called the heart, 'big mind' and the brain, 'little mind.' When you want knowledge, *think*; when you want deep knowing, allow it to unfold from the heart.

· DEVELOPING 'THE WITNESS' ·

There is a capacity in us that we need to cultivate if we are to live with awareness. This is the part of us that watches and is unmoved by the drama of life. Through the practice of awareness we begin to extricate ourselves from our self-imposed prison of unawareness. We can witness everything — even ourselves. Whereas before we were inside and everything and everyone else was outside, from the point of view of the witness we are simply a part of the whole. We can be witnesses to ourselves. We can stand back in consciousness and witness our own lives. The witness is always available to us and the more we practise, the more it develops.

· CLARITY AND FEAR ·

Clarity is often perceived as a threat. It is as if clarity has the power to shake the foundations of our lives and our security. Why should we be fearful? We are afraid because the structure we are trying to protect and preserve is already insecure. Clarity does not threaten our security and the idea that it does, is something we deceive ourselves about. There is no security in unawareness, confusion or manufacturing a false security and the illusion of safety.

When our inner structures begin to falter and we realize our lives are built on unstable foundations, our first impulse is to reinforce them. When we do this, we are fooling ourselves. For example, when a friend or partner asks us for reassurance which we feel we cannot honestly give, we may feel that we have to refuse. We have to make the same kind of decision in our own lives. We can either fear insecurity or welcome it. Alan Watts advised us to do more than welcome insecurity; he encouraged us to become it:

> To stand face to face with insecurity is still not to understand it. To understand it, you must not face it but be it.[8]

Embracing our fundamental insecurity allows our spontaneous and vivid sense of life to return – a life which may have been lost to us for a long time.

I stood in the middle of the room. Two facilitators – one male and one female – were on either side of me howling into my ears. A friend stood directly in front of me, also screaming at me. About fifteen people sat around the edges of the room. I was only dimly aware of them. I had a very effective character defence of arrogance, veiled mental aggression and complete denial of my emotional life based on historical pain and emotional abandonment. Personal growth groups had fascinated me. I had finally participated in one and 'got angry' – which was a great experience for me, but I had never really opened up or let down my defences before and, of course, I was terrified to do so. Either out of exasperation or compassion, my friend and the facilitators had decided it was time to lever me out of myself with a triple assault. They screamed at me to let go, to feel something – anything – to open up. I began to breathe faster and deeper, faster and deeper and then... Suddenly all the ranting and cajoling got through my shell and penetrated my vital core and I found myself standing in the middle of the room wailing like a baby, wailing with such deep feelings of loss and abandonment, longing and need... waves and waves of intense and overwhelming feeling filled me and poured through me, my body crumpled and shaking... for perhaps twenty minutes or more I cried and cried and couldn't see through the tears. The waves stopped gradually and naturally. I opened my eyes and began to look out into the room. Everyone was seated around me and they and the windows and the light streaming into the room, the coloured cushions, the wooden floor – all seemed to have taken on a sheen of the most amazing, vivid luminosity. Everything was more vivid, more beautiful and full of vibrant life. This was how the world had looked before I had stored up all those feelings inside which had deadened me.

·THE HEART AND THE MOMENT: INSIGHT AND HEALING·

Insight and understanding grow out of expanded awareness, which is attained through patient and persistent meditation. The experience of insight is impossible to put into words. As you deepen into the moment and the clouds clear, you become the endless sky. As you become less and less concerned with the content of your awareness and more freely engaged in the process; the mind opens. When the mind opens like this, you connect with and open in the heart – a heart that was previously contracted by the mind's worries, anxieties and fears. The heart is receptive to insight. The heart is where you are happy and free. Insight is the experience of simple and profound being. It is beyond words.

Healing and awareness take place in the moment. As soon as you find you are thinking about being aware, it is gone. Let us look at 'the moment'. Have you ever asked yourself, 'Why can't I be in the moment? What's the problem if that's where true life is?' When you try to do an awareness exercise, why do you so easily fail? You think about breakfast or lunch and even if you are thinking, 'I'm doing it now', you have lost it. Even the most insignificant matter claiming your attention results in the loss of your awareness. Your resistance is almost total. You spend the whole time just noticing that you cannot succeed in being aware. It is very humbling. If the secret is coming into this moment – and you are present physically, emotionally and mentally – what is the problem?

The reason is that absolutely everything of the self is clustered around the moment. When you think of a moment, it sounds so small, almost insignificant, but it is no little thing. All the enemies of awareness – projections, unfinished business, judgements and delusion – are clustered around the moment. As you begin to deepen your awareness, feelings come up – anger, shame, self-blame, hate – all those negative feelings that you have disavowed. Every emotional state that you can possibly think of, that you have buried, projected and avoided, is thickly clustered around the moment. As you approach the moment, these feeling states rise closer to the surface. If you could release all these feelings right now, then you would enter this moment. No longer would you have those powerful feelings so closely coiled around the very tiny essence of yourself that has been buried deep inside you. Your truth would be set free. As you released the feelings, you would start to feel more real, because you would come closer to the moment.

When you start to live with your feelings, it is an indication that you are getting closer. Most people spend their lives pushing feelings away. The more intense your feelings become, the closer you are getting to yourself. Resistance arises because of previous successions of moments that were so painful, and experiences that were threatening to you, that the only way to survive was through protection and defence until, finally, your defences totally eclipsed the moment. So when your intention is to be in the moment, you face a dense layer of emotional defences. Your way of protecting yourself from the pain has been to build up all these layers around you. You are deeply hidden, but your true self remains intact.

Each moment is precious and unique. The opportunities it contains may never come again; so do not waste your moments. Each opportunity taken moves you further along your spiritual path and closer to truth.

· AWARENESS AND EXPERIENCE ·

The world we experience is simply a series of phenomena, arising and dissolving. You can look around you and see a man, a woman, a car, a flower and if you can treat them all as phenomena, you will experience great acceptance. You might find it easier to appreciate the aesthetic sense of a daffodil than a pile of washing-up; but each is just a phenomenon, no better or worse than anything else.

A phenomenon is what is *in itself*, without attaching the projections of mind. The concept of phenomena is a helpful tool in your awareness practice. There are no 'better' or 'worse' people or things. Awareness is all there is.

The models we lay over experience inhibit natural awareness. We create a complex scenario with everything set up in a pre-modelled relationship to everything else – where we are, what we are doing, what classification each thing fits into, what is good and bad. This can be so dense and so tightly controlled that you cannot truly experience anything. Everything that exists for you is contained within your model and you cannot see anything which exists outside of it. How can you penetrate your resistance, transcend your models and simply experience life?

Many years ago I booked to participate in an Enlightenment Intensive – a powerful group-event for spiritual growth. I had never taken part in this particular group format before, although I had always wanted to. So I drove to the venue – a rural, community house – feeling a strong mixture of relief and excitement. It felt very much like the right time for me to be doing this. When

Warriors who deliberately attain total awareness are a sight to behold. That is the moment when they burn from within. The fire from within consumes them. And in full awareness they fuse themselves to the emanations of the Eagle at large, and glide into eternity.

Carlos Castaneda

I arrived I found that the group had been cancelled. I was the only person who had booked and they had forgotten to write and tell me. All my expectations and models dissolved. I felt angry and resentful. The collapse of my model – of how I expected things to be – was devastating. Yet something inside yielded and, as I adapted to the changing conditions and worked through my heated reactions to my disappointment, I was able to accept the community members' invitation to stay and enjoy the atmosphere of the place.

Afterwards, I began to see other people's models quite clearly. The weight of tightly held opinions and fixed expectations became very obvious to me. Some people's models were so constricting that they circumscribed their lives. Whatever models they held designed the creation of any situation. Their motivation dictated the form of their experience. When they sought something outside their normal frame of reference, they set up an impossible barrier. Either they became so attached to their seeking that nothing would satisfy them; or they would convince themselves they had found what they were seeking, until the seeker in them regained the upper hand again.

Controlling your experience with fixed models and expectations stifles spontaneity and excitement. When you relax your control, life can be full of surprises and unexpected opportunities.

• AWARENESS IS ETERNAL •

Awareness is far greater than self-identity. The thought that is 'I', which obsesses us so much, and the succession of thoughts that give the illusion of substance to our separate selves, are constantly dying in our awareness. Like a droplet of water momentarily suspended and separated from the torrent of a waterfall, the thoughts creating the self are disengaged from awareness, while awareness is eternally present. Through gentle and persistent effort in practising awareness, we draw further towards our knowing and cultivate the witness. We change from *practising* awareness to *being* awareness.

Practising awareness unites us with all spiritual power, because our natural state is awareness. We touch the Higher Self whenever we practise awareness. We grow clearer and keener in our relationship to the world of the senses. We fulfil and transcend the world of the senses and move into the realms of the spirit. We become perfect witnesses to truth. We are at one with the truth of the Self and everything is unified in the Self. We are already what we truly are, and have always been so.

There was a fish who went to a queen fish and asked, 'I have always heard about the sea, but what is this sea? Where is it?'

The queen fish explained, 'You live, move, and have your being in the sea. The sea is within you and without you, and you are made of sea, and you will end in sea. The sea surrounds you as your own being.'[9]

Where is the sea? Where is enlightenment? Where is the Self? Where is God? These questions are all the same question. The answer is nowhere and everywhere. The world is alive within you. When you are awareness you realize the world.

LESSENING

All know that the drop merges into the ocean, but few know that the ocean merges into the drop.

Ramana Maharshi

We build up so much around ourselves, bolstered as we are with opinions, glowing with self-importance, inflated with ego, polished with ability, defended with aggression. Deep within us, our essence – pure, simple and profound – waits to be discovered. This discovery takes our courage, commitment and trust. We must be brave enough to peel off all that is unreal, all that obscures the true self, and all that defends the imaginary 'I' from imaginary attack. By the clear light of awareness, we pierce the veils of projection and illusion, allowing all that is false to fall away. We peel off layers of self until we are at the empty centre, which is at the heart of our creation. This is the process of lessening.

In lessening, you see through and shed your attachment to your identity. As you release your attachment, you create more inner space. You have to work at tolerating this space. This inner 'emptiness' becomes the womb of spiritual transformation. Emptying yourself of attachments and tolerating the space are the two main themes of this stage. In this stage we look at peeling off the layers, illusions and self worth, animus possession, transcendence and waiting.

·PEELING OFF THE LAYERS·

Awareness reveals the self; lessening diminishes the self. We are not who we think we are and we must face the disparity between our self-image and our real Self. Through awareness and lessening we let go of the unreal and accept the real. For a while our new and old models of self 'slide' against each other and create dissonance. When we finally shed the illusory, what remains is truth.

As we deepen in our awareness practice and dissolve our models, expectations and judgements fall away. We become more simple and more clear. We see things as they are, without adorning them with the endless creations of our mind.

The unreal never is: the Real never is not. This truth indeed has been seen by those who can see the true.[1]

Gently we peel away the layers of the false self and, as each one is peeled away, we draw nearer to our heart, closer to our centre and truer to ourselves. The peeling and shedding of layers flow naturally and effortlessly from our spiritual practice. The light of awareness withers everything that is false, insincere and dishonest in us. As we continue in our practice we connect to our true self, which is beyond the fluctuation of truth and lies. Deep within us is a natural ethos: without separation what we do to others we do to ourselves. External morality always wears the hue of oppression and gives rise to duty, coercion and guilt. Here at our deepest centre we discover the true nature of relationship and it is the way of love, compassion and unity.

As the layers of the self are peeled away we create inner space. This 'emptiness' is our spiritual challenge now. How can we be with this new state of spaciousness? People who are beginning inner work are conspicuous in my workshops. They are uncomfortable sitting still, enduring the silences and the lack of action. They may not have sat still for so long during their entire lives! Yet out of this space come experiences that are more profound and fulfilling than anything we could do to interrupt the stillness or to fill the silence.

We have to develop our ability to tolerate silence, stillness and emptiness because it is very easy to clear out some of the *maya* – the deceptive, illusory appearance of things – and then fill it back in again. Even if we fill it in with thoughts such as, 'Now I'm really getting somewhere,' or, 'Now, I'm really becoming my true self,' we are resisting the emptiness that we have created through lessening. We have to work at holding the space open inside so that there is more of us available. This is a deeply challenging and profound aspect of spiritual practice.

· TAKING OFF YOUR MASK ·

As we begin to peel off the layers, we become more vulnerable and we may feel threatened. Our ego has constructed a defensive mask around our true self and that mask is starting to come away. A voice inside screams, 'If you keep tinkering around, your defence programme may not work anymore and then you

We hardly ever realize that we can cut anything out of our lives, anytime, in the blink of an eye.

Carlos Castaneda

will really get hurt.' We can go through a decline, feel lost, confused, or depressed. We may feel less than when we started and find, as Joseph Campbell put it, that we have climbed the ladder only to find that it is up against the wrong wall.[2] Fear can take over. Real change is beckoning; habit is holding us back. This process can manifest itself as confusion, depression, losing our grip, missing appointments or deadlines, emotional outbursts, sleepless nights or lapses in concentration. We need time and space to re-evaluate everything as the old internal structures crumble and we move on in the process of transformation.

The poet Robert Bly calls this 'ashes time'.[3] You feel worse than ever. This is the experience of pointlessness and despair. All the motivations and drives that you have felt in your life are being re-examined and reassessed. If your inner self sheds them, what will become of you? Instead of overlaying something else on top of it, accept that this is 'ashes time', and go down inside yourself and allow your feelings to take their course. The layers are peeling off, leaving you feeling raw, and your worst nightmares are appearing. In these conditions do not expect too much of yourself in the outer world. Do not expect yourself to function in the ways you are used to.

Ask yourself, 'Do I really need to hold on so tightly to get through the day? Do I really need to approach another person with so much suspicion just in case they reject me?' Life holds so many possibilities and we spend such a lot of time preparing ourselves for them. We become so defended by our preparations that we miss the opportunities for the living relationships and spontaneous opportunities that are before us in any given moment. We need to let go of the preparations so that the true self can emerge.

Virtually no one can undertake the spiritual journey to completion without an intimate confidant and guide. This confidant may be in the role of therapist, counsellor, teacher, priest, mentor, or friend. In lessening, more than at any other time, you need someone as a fixed star. Your world is changing so fast; you need someone to reflect off; someone who can anchor you in your feelings, thoughts and experiences. Your guide should appreciate your spiritual path, be open and attentive to you and not personally invested in the outcome of your journey.

·Four Essential Practices·

There are four essential practices for deep inner work – trust yourself, be curious, take risks, and find out for yourself. These practices encourage your wise, open, courageous and authentic self to develop.

First, trust yourself and trust what you experience, follow your own wisdom and guidance. There are subtle ways of giving your trust over to someone else and the result is always to disempower you. You should never trust someone more than you trust yourself and you should never forsake your own wisdom for somebody else's. Always return to your wisdom and to its source inside you.

Second, be curious. Watch yourself – your behaviour, thoughts, feelings, reactions, and resistances. You can learn everything about yourself, even from the smallest thing. Try and transcend your likes and your dislikes – the judgemental mind – and stay open. Develop your will, your openness, and surrender to learning from life. Most of all, cultivate your curiosity.

Third, take risks. You need your courage to take risks and to work at your 'edge'. Your edge is the point that you are in the process of going beyond. It is where your fear lives. It is what you do not want to talk about, the feeling that you are denying, or the decision that you are avoiding. The reason it is so important to work at your edge is that this is where the new shoots appear and it is from here that new growth will flourish.

Finally, find out for yourself so that your wisdom lives in your authentic self. Never simply accept what others tell you, however wise and trustworthy they may appear. Dare to trust yourself and your experience, rather than any external authority. Question and enquire, always be curious and open to the new. Follow your own intuition and create your own sense of meaning. Have your own experiences and live fully.

Consider these four practices whenever you feel lost or confused.

·TRANSCENDENCE·

Because the Divine is beyond ordinary reality, the spiritual traditions of the world point to the need to transcend the conditions of spatial-temporal existence. But the transcendence we seek is an inner condition, not an outer removal. This inner transcendence does not necessarily imply a conflict between spiritual and material values. Spiritual materialism may be expressed as much in material denial as by material enslavement. It is not a question of what, or how much, you have in your life, but of how you relate to what you have. The transcendence necessary is an inner state of essential indifference to the vicissitudes of worldly existence. We should expect nothing and be worthy of everything, as in this Zen saying:

> To keep the Way, resting at ease in poverty, is the basic lot of the wearer of the patchwork robe. Those who change their devotion because of destitution or success, gain or loss, are simply not yet worthy of talking to about the Way.[4]

We may turn to spirituality out of desperation and just as quickly drop it when our fortunes begin to improve. The spiritual journey demands our constancy, regardless of outer conditions. The pursuit of pleasure is perhaps the most challenging attachment to transcend. Those things that give us comfort from day to day can be the most poignant attachments that we have. During his incarceration by the Nazis, Jacques Lusseyran wrote:

> Among all the dangers that beset me, there would always be that one to reckon with, the one that comes from the enjoyment of everyday things.[5]

Driven inwards, both physically and psychologically, Lusseyran found his enjoyment of everyday things the most persistently dangerous. Why? Because he had discovered that joy turned into sorrow, then back again. His desire for joy was equal to his aversion to sorrow and both conditions threatened his survival. Loving or hating, wanting or not wanting – it was his attachment to any pair of opposite states that he had to let go of to be free.

Spiritual transcendence is going beyond the personal self. Transcendence is inner: we transcend to the essence within. This is true of all outer relationships that are projected aspects of our inner wholeness. When essence recognizes essence, there is a true meeting of souls. The ancient *Upanishads* say:

It is not for the love of a husband that a husband is dear; but for the love of the Soul in the husband that a husband is dear.

It is not for the love of a wife that a wife is dear; but for the love of the Soul in the wife that the wife is dear.

It is not for the love of children that children are dear; but for the love of the Soul in children that children are dear.

It is not for the love of all that all is dear; but for the love of the Soul in all that all is dear.[6]

Lessening brings us closer to our essence through an inner process of transcendence. We lessen ourselves until we see within. We transcend the world of appearances until we discern the Divine as the 'breath inside the breath',[7] the Self inside the self, the essential Reality.

· ILLUSIONS AND SELF WORTH ·

The lessons of lessening form an aspect of the spiritual journey that is very difficult to 'sell'. Most popular books on spiritual awakening either underplay or conceal these lessons. But lessening is a crucial stage of spiritual growth. Like the sleeping seed in the winter ground, although nothing appears to be happening, quiet, ceaseless and fundamental processes are taking place. Lessening is the gradual loss of all that we have gained that is false. When you feel the pain of this loss, ask, 'Who is feeling this pain?' If you find the experience of loss comes and goes, then it is not your true Self. The following passage was written almost a hundred years ago, but it has lost none of its relevance today.

We study the way not of acquiring but of losing. If one could acquire things at once, the system [of spiritual realisation] would be popular. But nothing can be promised. It is difficult to expect people to like this, for no one likes to lose illusions. People want positive things without realising what is possible. They want to know straight away what they can attain. But first they must lose many things. The ideas of this system can never be popular so long as they are not distorted, because people will not agree that they are asleep... people who consider themselves important will always oppose this idea.[8]

Self-importance is a construction of the ego and the ego likes to add to itself. Self-importance also hides our unworthiness and this is an aspect of our mask. We have to lose our attachment to self-importance and to unworthiness. Stephen Levine says:

> It's not uncommon for the sense of unworthiness to become more distinct, and seem like it's gotten worse, as awareness deepens... We let go of our sense of unworthiness not by submitting it to the axe or trying to control or suppress it, but by giving it enough room to see its own workings... We are worthy of letting go of our unworthiness. If we did nothing but practice letting go of unworthiness, much of the stuff we're working so hard to clear away would have no support system.[9]

Our ego structure hides our authentic self. The 'I' eclipses all that is important, all that is of value, all that is beautiful and wise. Our defences construct this contracted, little being around us – the egoic, separate self. Are we worthy enough to drop our defences? Do we think enough of ourselves? Our self worth is not our ego, our contraction, or our defences. Our self worth comes out of our inner emptiness, which is creative and beyond our perception of ourselves.

Your character hides the real you and your defences prevent you from meeting the world in a genuine way. To be real, this meeting requires a real world and a real you. Your self-importance is a mask that covers your unworthiness. Your unworthiness says you are not good enough to come out from behind your defences, and be just as you are.

·ANIMUS POSSESSION·

Women experience a special problem in working with self worth and it is what Jung called 'animus possession'.[10] Because we are deeply – most of us blindly – immersed in a patriarchal society, we have an egoic mask which is governed by patriarchal symbols and which supports the values of the patriarchy. This mask totally subdues a woman's true nature. So she has to find a way to remove the mask, because it denies her womanhood and the deep values of the feminine. Because patriarchy has established itself as the predominant structure in our culture, its principles and values have become embedded in our psyches. This aspect of the inner world of both men and women has been named the patripsych.[11] The patripsych upholds the values of the patriarchy unconsciously. While this poses a deep challenge for men, it creates a distinctly different problem for women.

A woman's conditioning is so imbued with male values that her ego structure relates exclusively to the male system and does not resonate with her natural female self. What makes this situation so difficult to work with is its unquestioned acceptance – not really seeing it, not knowing it, not thinking there is anything wrong with it, because rarely is any alternative perceived. So the difference for a woman is that as soon as you start to peel away the layers, what appears is an infantile layer of stunted growth that can be characterized as 'everything-that-pleases-daddy'. This is her deep and unquestioned conformity to the male value system. When that has been shed, there is this little seed or undeveloped impulse that is the tiny, unformed ego of her authentic femaleness waiting to be developed. Through these authentic female qualities a woman can re-engage with the world in an entirely new way.

Men too have to strip away their identification with the negative values of patriarchy, because a man's real potential is well hidden. So, for men, developing genuine self-worth is more of a humbling practice. When women engage in growth work they become more visible, more noisy and less civilized – more obviously free of cultural mores – whereas men tend to become more inward and more humble. It is a different direction, but for men as well as for women, the issue is finding out how much the patriarchy – unquestioned and inviolable – is within them.

A career woman has even more to handle with regard to the inner life. The higher she rises in the hierarchy of the man's world, the deeper she is subsumed in it. Do you know the story of the Greek goddess Athena? She was born out of a male version of a Caesarean section. While the god of heaven and earth, her father Zeus, screamed in agony, Hephaestus, the god of the forge, cut open his head with an axe. Out of the wound Athena was born, wearing full armour and brandishing weapons. She considered herself to have only one parent – her father Zeus. A professionally successful woman who is 'straight out of her daddy's head', functions not from her femininity, but from the patripsych within her. The Jungian analyst Sylvia Brinton Perera writes movingly on the split psyche of the 'daughters of the patriarchy':

> The problem is that we who are badly wounded in our relation to the feminine usually have a fairly successful persona, a good public image. We have grown up as docile, often intellectual, daughters of the patriarchy, with what I call 'animus-egos'. We strive to uphold the virtues and aesthetic ideals that the patriarchal superego has presented to us. But we are filled with self-loathing and a deep sense of personal ugliness and failure when we can neither meet nor mitigate the superego's standards of perfection.[12]

Exploring the tension between male and female values leads you to another schism – the division between inner and outer. The repression of the in-turning, feminine principle by the outgoing, masculine principle is reflected in the history of war, conquest and gynocide – the destruction of women.[13] In dreams, the oppressive male figure, the dark man coming after you, represents the patriarchy and the oppressive masculine ego inside you saying, 'No, little girl!' This is the fear, the patriarchy personified and deeply internalized.

·A Time of Waiting·

Lessening is a challenging stage. It presages the dark night of the soul, the surrender of illusion, and the genuine deepening into truth. It is essential preparation for all that is to come. It is a time of waiting and of tolerating waiting, of self-nourishment and developing clarity.

T.S.Eliot captured the state of fecund emptiness that is the outcome of profound lessening:

> I said to my soul, be still, and wait without hope
> For hope would be hope for the wrong thing; wait without love
> For love would be love of the wrong thing; there is yet faith

But the faith and the love and the hope are all in the waiting.
Wait without thought, for you are not ready for thought:
So the darkness shall be the light, and the stillness the dancing...
...to arrive at what you are not
You must go through the way in which you are not...
In my end is my beginning.[14]

Lessening heralds the dawn of re-enchantment, new buds of wonder in our lives. Do not shrink from it, do not hurry it, do it fully.

OPENING

But this detachment must not be mere amputation; everything which is shaken off must be simultaneously found again at a higher level.

Gabriel Marcel

The work we do on ourselves becomes our gift to everybody else, because the clearer you are, the more your heart is open, the quieter you are, the more you've become an environment through which other people can become free because less and less do you need anything from them and you're more just present with the moment.

Ram Dass

As you learn to be with the emptiness that arises out of your awareness, practice, so you begin to open in an entirely new way. You are creating the space inside you into which the world can now enter and reveal itself. You are creating the kind of emptiness that can hear, receive and resonate with sense experience, with another person, and with the Divine. There is an interchange, making relationship possible between self and other.

In this stage we consider life statements and divine lessons, working with fear, subpersonalities and making decisions, relationships and intimacy, working with the body and practising openness. It is only when we are open to the generosity of life that we can receive its gifts. Opening is characterized by the spirit of curiosity, questioning and recognizing fear, resistance and contraction within.

•LIFE STATEMENTS: TRUNKS AND BRANCHES•

The key to our resistance to opening to a full relationship with life lies in our conditioning. We store memories and feelings deep inside ourselves and live our lives in the scant inner space which remains. We have to work with these deeply held beliefs that determine our characters and construct our inner world.

Life statements are the distillation of the negative messages that we received from our early environment. They are a combination of how we believed others felt about us and how we felt about ourselves. Of the many and various life statements that we adopt, there are two core statements – 'I'm worthless', and 'I'm bad'. 'I'm worthless' lies at the core of issues of self-esteem. 'I'm bad' reflects deep issues of shame and blame. Usually we are attached to one of these statements, depending on the emphasis of the disapproval – implied or explicit – in our early lives. Our life statements dictate our patterns and unconsciously direct our lives, keeping us small and closed. They are the primary psychological causes of our repression.

Growing out of our core life statements are branch life statements. Some examples are: 'I don't belong here'; 'There's nobody there for me'; 'I don't need anyone'; 'I do everything wrong'; 'I have to work to be alright'; 'My feelings are unacceptable'.

Our life statements numb us to our pain and conceal our deep wounds. But the wounds conceal divine lessons. If you can just see past the individual injustice, hurt, sorrow, shame, neglect, denial – the trunk and the branches – and ask, 'What have these experiences taught me?' then you begin to see the lessons in your wounds.

One of my life statements was, 'Life is a struggle'. It had its roots in my birth experience when my survival depended on my ability to keep on fighting and not give in. I had not realized that I was choosing to live my life as a struggle because I had always experienced my life through a veil of struggle. I knew no other way. Needing life to struggle against had disadvantages. I habitually used effort whether or not effort was needed; I was unable to sustain good relationships because I was unconsciously seeking out conflict; when life became easy I would sabotage it. When I understood, I was able to see what the life statement, 'Life is a struggle', was costing me and choose a different way.

Work with your life statements, write them down, learn to recognize them as they arise. Life statements are continually present and they direct your life. It is crucial that you keep them in your awareness because they only continue to exist by avoiding the spotlight of the inner eye. As they work stealthily behind your consciousness, there is a powerful compulsion to ignore them. You need to bring your life statements into your consciousness and assert, 'I am not

When experience is viewed in a certain way, it presents nothing but doorways into the domain of the soul.

Jon Kabat-Zinn

going to be controlled by these beliefs. This does not tell me how the world is, just how the world was. This is how I learnt to handle the conditions of my early life'.

You can work on your life statements by reversing them. Compose the antidote and put it into practice. For example, 'It's all my fault' becomes 'It's not all my fault', 'Life is a struggle' becomes 'Life is easy', 'I'm not good enough' becomes 'I'm fine just as I am', 'I have to be strong for other people' becomes 'I can let others look after me'.

Branch life statements often conceal hidden abilities and discovering these abilities can clarify your life direction. For example, if you have a statement like, 'I don't fit in', you could work very well with marginalized groups because of your deep empathy with them. If you have a statement like, 'Life is hard', you could be capable of tasks of great endurance, since hard challenges would be second nature to you. If you have a statement like, 'I don't want to be here', you may have great gifts of imagination and be drawn to art or literature. If you work through your life statements, you can liberate the latent talents they conceal; but while the life statements remain unexplored, these talents tend to remain concealed.

Life statements are self-fulfilling. The power of the unconscious is such that if we are carrying the life statement, 'I don't want to be here', we can affect the people around us who may experience the reactive statement, 'I don't want you here'. If we carry the life statement, 'My feelings are unacceptable', we will be most likely to choose a partner who does not accept our feelings. If we carry the life statement, 'If I do better, then I will be loved', we usually choose relationships in which love is conditional. In this way our life statements justify themselves and life fulfils our negative expectations.

·WORKING WITH FEAR·

There is nothing 'wrong' with any emotional state. Each emotional state is simply a manifestation of energy. If we develop our awareness of emotions as energy, we can redirect the energy by reinterpreting and disconnecting it from the interpretation that our mind has made. For example, on a physiological level fear and excitement are the same, and so too are laughing and crying. As we react to certain stimuli, the mind is busy forming an interpretation that is in keeping with its expectations according to our personal story, life statements and psychological patterns. Usually the energetic level is eclipsed by the interpretation of our mind. By becoming aware of the energetic level, and watching the unfolding as it occurs, we expand our understanding of feeling as manifestations of energy. Eventually, we are able to witness it as an energetic process, which was veiled by the mind's interpretation.

In the West, most of us are physically comfortable and secure, so fear is mainly generated internally as anxiety. Choosing fear keeps us small. We might not be aware that we are choosing fear, but fear is part of our deep conditioning and its contracting effect has become habitual. When we explore how fear emerges in our consciousness we discover exactly how we choose it.

Spiritually, fear is the opposite of love. Physiologically and psychologically fear is our reaction to danger. When we live our lives in fear, we become destructive as we react against a world of perceived threat. Love becomes the casualty, since love and fear cannot co-exist.

We need not be afraid of fear. Fear contracts and prevents us from opening. We can transform it by finding the courage to 'inhabit' fear when it arises, by feeling the process of contraction – the pulling away, the smallness and the defeat. When we place our awareness within fear like this it does not act against us because we have not separated ourselves from it. This is how we discover the real nature of fear. Ken Wilber writes:

> In this war between opposites, there is only one battleground – the human heart. And somehow, in a compassionate embrace of the dark side of reality, we become bearers of the light. We open to the other – the strange, the weak, the sinful, the despised – and simply through including it, we transmute it. In doing so, we move ourselves towards wholeness.[1]

When we reach the level at which fear is simply energy, we can transform it. We can work with anger, pain, sorrow, shame and all other emotional states in exactly the same way, bringing awareness to them and transforming them at an energetic level.

·Yes and No·

Most decisions are made unconsciously and are habitually fixed in their nature. Understanding how we make decisions provides us with new opportunities for openness. Noticing when we say 'yes' and when we say 'no' can tell us a great deal about ourselves. How do we decide between 'yes' and 'no'? What is the feeling of 'yes' and of 'no'?

We do ourselves a great disservice in expecting the self to be consistent and single-minded, because we are made up of different subpersonalities. We need to find expression for our selves, rather than for our self. Decisions always illumine our subpersonalities, because we have to decide which part of us will mediate the inner process; which parts will be allowed to affect the decision and which parts will be sidelined.

Within us there is a kind of council meeting of parts and the question is who will affect the decision and the outcome – the child or the adult, the conformist or the dissenter, the ego or the Higher Self?

The ego is at the centre of our consciousness; the Higher Self is at the centre of our wholeness, which is inclusive of both consciousness and the unconscious. When we make a decision out of our ego, we appear to know exactly what we are doing and why we are doing it. When we allow a decision to be made out of the Higher Self, we may be unsure of ourselves. Yet I have found that the latter is the wiser way.

Whenever I am faced with a problem or a proposition, many subpersonalities emerge in response. There are many different points of view inside me – some argue for, others against; some harmonize, others conflict; some compromise, others confuse; some are knowing and others not knowing. I try to acknowledge and listen to them all, without following my attachments, until this inner activity calms down. Then I notice my ego's preference and try to let that go too. Eventually, an answer emerges and, most often, that answer is to say 'yes' to the situation. This 'yes' represents openness to life. It is the sound of life itself. In the ancient *Upanishads*, inner and outer Truth are the same – Brahman is Atman – and the sacred syllable OM is the name for both. One of the meanings of OM is 'yes'. This 'yes' to life expresses the willingness to be a part of the greater whole and to participate in unified Consciousness.

·OFFERING UP·

Sometimes life overwhelms us and we are unable to make the 'right' decision or see our way through a difficult situation. At times like these we need to recognize the limitations of the small, separate self and open up to help from a higher level. Offering up is giving back the ultimate responsibility for our lives to the Eternal. It is opening up to our Higher Self and asking for help.

If our sense of well-being lies no deeper than our small separate self and the changing conditions of life, then we will not be truly happy. Life presents us with so many causes of happiness. Yet setback, failure, disappointment, disillusionment and conflict are facts of life. We have good days and bad days. But anxiety can make us unhappy all the time, whether experiencing adverse circumstances or in anticipation of them. Change is certain, as are good and bad days, but if, instead of identifying with them, we can deepen in our awareness to how things are, then we can be happy behind the ever-changing conditions of life. We can watch the clouds go by and remain in spacious awareness.

Do you remember the times in your life when fortuitous things simply happened which led you into significant life changes? You did not sit down and plan the route or the changes, did you? If you look back at your life and see how new opportunities arose, they probably did not have much to do with decision making. You did not know why you happened to be in a particular place at a particular time in your life, but you were there and you said 'yes'. How did you get in touch with the key people in your life or make the decisions that brought you to this present moment?

Old people sometimes can look back on their lives with a broad vision. They see that the sequence of apparently random, arbitrary or chance encounters and circumstances that made up their earlier life reflects an intelligent pattern of events, rich in learning and purpose. Providence appears as a benign force. Offering up gives providence a chance to act in our lives.

·HANDLING REALITY AND NOT KNOWING·

We can abandon our bodies in one of two basic ways; by withdrawing inwards or escaping outwards. In these times of intense self-consciousness, we have created a third way – we retreat from the psychologically intolerable within, while maintaining the appearance of 'being here.' This defence is much less direct than simply running away or retreating as a way of handling reality. We perform a 'sleight-of-hand', by disassociating our minds from our bodies. It is a peculiar predicament, a defence of profound denial – we are here, yet not here.

Nudge open your personal defences a little bit and challenge your closedness. What is your habitual form of avoiding reality? Do you run away, fight, or flee inwards to escape meeting the world? As you become familiar with your defences, be gentle and do not judge. At first, try peeking out a little, just testing the water. Next, as you get to know how you protect yourself, you might feel confident enough to come out, when you are sure it is safe. Eventually, you may choose to meet the world in openness, without any certainties, allowing yourself to not know. The ability to not know allows the space for wisdom to come in. Stephen Levine says:

> We're constantly building a new image of ourselves and wondering what's next. We have allowed ourselves very little space for not knowing. Very seldom do we have the wisdom not-to-know, to lay the mind open to deeper understanding... Confusion arises because we fight against our not knowing, which experiences each moment afresh without preconceptions or expectations.[2]

· RELATIONSHIPS AND 'RESCUING' ·

Human relationships can be threatened when real change brings about fresh expectations. But change is only a threat to a relationship which is already stagnating. A genuine relationship is alive and growing. Since change is integral to life, change cannot threaten a healthy relationship.

Relationships fail unless there is a strong sense of companionship, holding, mutual support and encouragement between partners. We may have to give up the role of 'rescuer' that is so common in our unconscious expectations of relationships. Not rescuing means allowing someone to learn from their experiences without our interference. We cannot take away another's pain. We must resist the temptation to do so, in the deeper knowledge that the pain is only a part of the experience, which will make them stronger, more realized beings.[3]

We may find that hidden beneath the compulsion to rescue is the desire to keep our friend, lover or spouse at a fixed level of development in which we feel secure with them. We cannot, however, resist the inevitable tides of change. Without change, life and relationships sink into decline. By encouraging growth and change, we keep our relationships healthy, alive and full of love.[4]

• TRUE INTIMACY •

The deep human yearning for true intimacy must first be fulfilled within oneself. We can only be as intimate with another as we can be with ourselves and by deepening in self-intimacy, we make it possible to invite the intimacy of another. The distance between ourselves and another is always the unfinished business we have with ourselves.

The word intimacy comes from the Latin, *intimitus*, and carries the original meaning of an announcement or an expression, as well as a sense of inner essence. Intimacy can be seen as the heart's announcement to the self – the relationship of self to soul, or of self to Self. Between two people, it is a relationship of trust and openness and the willingness to reveal our essential reality – who we really are – to each other. It is opening up and receiving another and being received. One of our deepest longings is to open up fully and have the other still be there for us. When someone offers us intimacy we should always respect it. But unreciprocated intimacy is a contradiction. If we are unable to return intimacy, we should be clear with the other about how we feel. On the ego level, many people live out the statement, 'If you really knew me, then you wouldn't love me'. It is vital to us that we are liked, so we manipulate ourselves, presenting and pretending to be what we think the other likes. This is the opposite of intimacy.

Genuine relationship requires a deep acceptance of the other. Each partner must choose the relationship as a vehicle for growth and be ready to make that choice – it is not enough simply to desire a growthful relationship. When you are ready, the other will appear:

On the day of my fortieth birthday, I found myself in a peat field in Southern Ireland on a rock surrounded by water. The water was so still and the sky so clear, I could see myself vividly in the mirror of the lake. I had just walked out of another relationship. I was full of blame, anger and resentment and, beneath that, I was feeling very foolish. I had been having disturbing fantasies about growing old and dying with no one to care about me. Over the next few weeks, I began to see this as a reflection of my own psyche. Within me was an oppressor, a saboteur who did not care about me, as well as a victim who felt guilty, but preferred to blame somebody else. The more I looked at the attempts at intimacy I had made through my life, the more confused and disastrous things appeared.

Nature seemed to me full of wonders, and I wanted to steep myself in them. Every stone, every plant, every single thing seemed alive and indescribably marvellous. I immersed myself in nature, crawled, as it were, into the very essence of nature...

Carl Jung

I needed time, so I decided to give myself a retreat. I rented a little cottage miles away from the nearest town and made the commitment to living with myself. Over the next few months, I grew to know myself in ways I had never known myself before. I discovered my energy cycles, what foods I liked to eat, the daily rhythms that most suited me, how emotional states arose in me (with no one else to blame!) – what I was truly like.

The desolate experience of my fortieth birthday led me to a single focus of intention: I never wanted to cause hurt again. This became my guiding light. In the darkness of intense loneliness, in the burning of desire, through the murkiness of confusion and projection, I remained with myself. I ritualized severing the ties of past relationships. I grew intimate with myself as a life partner. I grew close to nature – wind, rain, sunshine, grass, moorland, the night and the dawn. I dreamed powerful dreams of wholeness and of higher realms.

One of the gifts I gave myself during this period was the opportunity to read the books I had been drawn to, but never found the time to read. The only excursions I made away from my cottage were to collect the books I had ordered from a small bookshop in the nearby town. One day I walked into the bookshop and there, standing in the shadows in a corner, was a beautiful, young woman whose soul spoke to me when our eyes met. She became my life partner and with her I have experienced the deep intimacy and love I had always longed for.

·WORKING WITH THE BODY·

Your heart, your belly, and your pelvis are three of the primary energy centres in your body. Within each of these centres there is energetic, emotional and spiritual life. When you open up in these centres, you can harmonize and balance the energies and feelings that are there. Your heart is the centre for sorrow, longing, grief, love and compassion. Your belly is the centre for self-esteem, resentment, relationship issues, the material world and the physical body. Your pelvis is the centre for power issues, sexuality, anger, aggression, assertiveness, creativity and grounding.

Invite your awareness into each of these centres in turn. Allow yourself to visualize, intuit, and sense the qualities in each one. Remember you *are* your heart, belly and pelvis, in the same way you have been taught that you are your mind. Each of these centres has 'intelligence' of its own. Any one of them reveals aspects of your body's wisdom. Your Intelligence is physical, emotional and spiritual as well as mental.

As you cultivate a relationship with your body and its energy centres, you challenge the power of the mind. The mind controls, whereas the body experiences. The body is more open than the mind, so you become less closed and more available when you experience yourself as body as well as mind.

Through the development of the heart, belly and pelvis we can reach balance and equanimity. We are the meeting of soulful and spiritual qualities. It is natural for us to be earthy and sensual, to relate to the earth and the physical manifestations of life. These ground and stabilize us. It is also in our nature to strive towards the spiritual, to reach upwards through thought and creativity, philosophy and contemplation. When these two combine, we experience a sense of wholeness.

Find an expression for your earthiness and your wildness. Find a way to express passion and ecstasy in your life, to enter a space in which you can forget yourself. It may be dance, music, nature, athletics, martial arts, mountain climbing, sensuality or sexuality – find out what it is for you. We have become too 'civilized' today. You have unbounded oceans of pleasure and excitement inside which you can share with others, share with yourself, grow from, expand into; so reaching the very depths of your soul. All it takes is your courage to be all that you are.

·The Practice of Opening·

There are four skills that are invaluable for opening and can be used effectively in your relationships with other people. They are acknowledgement, unconscious communication, empathy and resonance.

Someone who will sit and make eye contact and listen to you can be enough to satisfy you. This is because most of us are starved of genuine acknowledgement. For some people it is hard to bear. If you come from a family in which no one looks at, or listens to, anyone else, where you start to speak and somebody else cuts in with what they think, it is affirming and nourishing to be acknowledged. Eyes that see and ears that hear are profoundly healing. Offer acknowledgement to others and look for it in your friends. Looking and listening with openness, and truly receiving another, provides acknowledgement. It is an ability that we all possess.

We can be open to more than thought alone. If someone is talking to you and you are 'listening' with your whole self – body, mind and spirit – there can be another deeper communication of which they are unaware. This is unconscious communication. We give signals in our posture, our tone of voice and through our energy. At times, what is being said is less true than what is not being said. You cannot sense this through your rational mind; you pick it up intuitively in your body centres. 'Listening' is a full body experience which you have to practise and trust your body to do it.

The third skill, empathy, is a quality which is available to you when you are open. Energies flow through the body and any obstruction affects the energetic whole. For example, if you have cleared your heart and belly but your pelvis is blocked, your capacity for empathy is restricted. Work through your energetic body centres with breath and awareness to move and clear your energy. When your personal energy is flowing once again, it will clear and you can sense another's energy and feelings.

In the process of inner work there is a point where you feel a sense of completion. This sense of completion is like a journey around the self. You have realized the wholeness of your personality and found the edges of your egoic limits. At this point something important happens with empathy. You find yourself resonating with the feelings and conditions of others, yet this resonance does not depend upon your having had the same, or even similar, experiences. When you arrive at the edges of your ego, the self-imposed boundaries of personality are less defined. You can extend your consciousness further and be in resonance with another.

·TOTAL OPENNESS·

To end our discussion of opening, here is an account of an initiation into total openness. It is an exposition of the words of St. John of the Cross: 'To arrive at being all, desire to be nothing,' and of *A Course in Miracles*: 'I have invented the world I see.' It is cutting through illusion and seeing things as they are, opening to life and cultivating an inner emptiness where you can meet and experience life and truth. Behind the mind of forms, dreams, thoughts and ideas is the pure essence of mind – the Original Mind of Zen out of which form originates and whose quality is openness.

Soon after his arrival, Ramakrishna placed his right foot on Naren's body, and the effect was literally shattering. '... first of all I began to see that the houses – rooms, doors, windows, verandas – the trees, the sun, the moon – all were flying off – shattering to pieces as it were – reduced into atoms and molecules...' After that prelude, the next stage involved the complete destruction of the consciousness of being a separate self; it seemed that 'the entire universe was about to vanish into a vast, all-devouring void.' Naren thought he was dying and cried out in panic, 'What are you doing to me? I have my parents, brothers and sisters at home!' At this, Ramakrishna laughed and touched Naren's chest with his hand, at which the world returned little by little, and Naren again 'began to see the houses, doors, windows, verandas and other things'. More reassuring still, he came to himself... All his assumptions had been undermined and his mind paced up and down inside the cage of his conditioning, shaking its leonine head in fretful perplexity.[5]

· Part 3 ·

THE HIGHER SELF

POWER AND SURRENDER

Surrender to your own Self, of which everything is an expression.

Sri Nisargadatta Maharaj

... the way to success... is by 'surrender'... Give up the feeling of respon-
sibility, let go your hold, resign the care of your destiny to higher powers, be
genuinely indifferent as to what becomes of it all... It is but giving your lit-
tle private convulsive self a rest, and finding that a greater Self is there.

William James

As we move into the second half of the spiritual journey, we travel deeper into the unknown. We must now pass through the doorway between the personal and the universal, the human and the Divine. This is the surrender of one's own life to Life itself. Through this doorway the ordinary is extraordinary, the smallest thing is transcendent, and life is sacred once more. We are given life only to surrender it to its source in reverence. This reciprocity is the Divine agreement. The more we give, the more we receive. To commit to this agreement we have to remove all our excuses, avoidances and habitual confusion. The commitment must be made from a deep place inside ourselves, which is open, vital and full of longing for the Divine. Our enlightened Self is always available and is not dependent on personal development. When we see that, there are no excuses left.

For a real transformation there must be a direct and unveiled intervention from above; there would be neces- sary too a total submission and surrender of the lower consciousness, a cessation of its insistence, a will in it for its separate law of action to be completely annulled by transformation and lose all rights over our being.

Sri Aurobindo

In this stage we explore the process of sur- render and the relinquishment of personal power, the urgency of the spiritual journey, the role of the unconscious, the spiritual warrior, synchronicity, self-importance and goal-lessness.

·Spiritual Urgency·

In the seventies I had *darshan* – literally 'a seeing' – with a guru in India. While he was talking to me, I felt a deep compassion combined with a tremendous urgency in him. I felt as if he had seized me by the scruff of the neck and shook me. His whole demeanour was crying out, 'Wake up! Wake up now!' He spoke of my inner turmoil and confusion, which revolved around my relying on the rational mind and distrusting my intuitive heart. He spoke about spontaneity and beauty, which was both inspiring and sad for me, and he made me see that my personal concerns were merely secondary – just part of the passing drama of life – and that it was vital to wake up and to do it now!

We tend to lose this sense of urgency, the vital nature of spirituality, as we go off to courses, workshops, therapy and healing sessions, waiting for 'it' to happen. The only spiritual course is the one you are enrolled on *now*. It is Life. Spiritual transformation does not depend on personal development. You are in class now, so be here without reserve and with all your passion.

When we are awake we are unconcerned about the next moment. To be present, spontaneous and open, wholly in each moment and participating totally in life, is to be totally alive. The flower does not know what it will become when it is a seed, a tiny shoot, or a stem. There is no certainty, only existence, relationship and experience. When we commit ourselves to life and its unfolding, we are sure to be in the process of becoming ourselves.

·The Unconscious and the Light·

Jung talked about the powerful impulse of the unconscious to be born into the light of consciousness. Whenever we are off guard – asleep, daydreaming or unaware – the unconscious may send symbolic messages through dreams, imagination, and even accidents. We must surrender our attachment to the small, separate self if we want to expand beyond our limitations. Just as the unconscious has this impulse to be born into the light, so life has this urge to fulfil itself in us.

Just as the tiny seed in the ground growing towards the light does not know what it will become, neither will you know what you truly are, until you have found the courage to live your own life. To live your own life you need to live from your innermost core. Truth surrounds you and flows within you; truth is always here, waiting to be found. There is nothing for you to find out, because you are endlessly wise. All that is needed is for you to release your attachments, as Ram Dass remarks:

> The truth is everywhere. Wherever you are... you can see it through whatever vehicle you are working with, you can free yourself from certain attachments that keep you from seeing it... You find how to do the things to yourself which allow you to find truth where you are at the moment... there's no invention, there is just discovery... we never find out anything new; we just remember it.[1]

Remembering ourselves requires descent and surrender. The meeting of the conscious and unconscious realities within us leads to wholeness, which is the fundamental nature of the Divine. Douglas Harding observed:

> The whole man is the Whole: nothing less is viable. However you look at him, then, whether from inside or outside, he is (in the last resort) that all-inclusive One which organises the diverse wills of all its members into One will which we call God's will – which is none other than your will when you know Who you really are and what you really want, when you are all there and wholly yourself.[2]

·SURRENDERING TO THE SELF·

Why is surrendering to the Self so difficult? Is it because we feel it is, in some sense, a defeat? Is it because we cannot get past the idea of surrendering to something other than, and opposed to, ourselves? A better way of understanding it is to see that we are surrendering to ourselves. We are not surrendering to God in heaven because there is never any distance between the Divine and ourselves. We are surrendering to the Higher Self, to God within. What makes us unwilling to surrender our wholeness to who we really are?

We have learnt not to trust. We do not trust ourselves and we do not trust others, because they carry the projections of our own untrustworthiness. We do not trust because we are confused and we are confused because we think we are our minds. The mind is the control centre, the director of our lives. In our minds there is a genius and a lunatic, a hero and a coward, a fool and a sage, amongst a diverse crowd of characters. They are within each one of us, but they are, neither collectively nor individually, all that we are.

What happens if you shift your centre to your heart? Shifting your centre from your head to your heart requires surrender. Courage is needed to surrender to the heart, which is your true Self. Ramana Maharshi said:

> Concentrating the mind solely on the Self will lead to happiness or bliss. Drawing in the thoughts, restraining them and preventing them from straying outwards is called detachment. Fixing them in the Self is spiritual practice. Concentrating on the heart is the same as concentrating on the Self. Heart is another name for Self.[3]

The heart is where we find our fire and our passion. The word courage is derived, through Middle English and Old French, from the Latin word *cor*, which means heart. Our thoughts do not transform anything because we cannot experience courage in our mind; we can only think about it. Thoughts may inspire the heart, but real courage must be felt in the heart. Surrendering to the Divine is synonymous with moving into the heart and becoming who we really are.

·THE PSYCHOLOGICAL ADULT AND THE SPIRITUAL WARRIOR·

The spiritual warrior is a symbol that can be found in most spiritual traditions. The Buddhist temple guardians (known as 'Thunderbolt Carriers') of Japan, the Old Testament prophet Isaiah, Castaneda's Don Juan, the Zen patriarch Bodhidharma and John the Baptist are just a few examples. These figures embody the rare quality of loving ferocity – inner strength, gentleness, courage, clarity and absolute commitment – which is vital for the spiritual journey.

The spiritual journey is not for undeveloped human beings. We will not get very far on the path of the spirit, unless we are willing to shed child-like or adolescent ego trappings. Jack Kornfield writes:

Many people first come to spiritual practice hoping to skip over their sorrows and wounds, the difficult areas of their lives. They hope to rise above them and enter a spiritual realm full of divine grace, free from all conflict... [But] as soon as practitioners relax in their discipline they again encounter all the unfinished business of the body and heart that they had hoped to leave behind.[4]

The spiritual journey is a complex undertaking and definitely not an escape. You must persistently renew your commitment, and overcome the traps and the perils that await you. You must embrace good and evil, ugliness and beauty, joy and misery, and use all of it to grow. John Welwood writes:

To be fully present to our experience as it is, without shrinking or turning away from it, is to be a warrior of the heart... To be a warrior of the heart means welcoming whatever arises in relationships, no matter how difficult or challenging, as an opportunity to grow stronger, to call forth new inner resources.[5]

The spiritual warrior is that part of you that roots out dishonesty and cuts through illusion to find truth. Its armour is openness and its strength lies in yielding. Its sword cuts through every kind of falsehood; its method lies in not knowing, never assuming, and surrender. It is alertness and integrity in action. It will check you, listen to you, and reflect back and be totally clear with you. It is unassailable because it is truly of the heart. Cultivate this part of you and have the courage to risk being authentic and spontaneous.

· THE SPINNING-TOP ·

Picture a spinning-top in motion – whirling and tilting. The still point is the central axis; all else is dizzy movement. Towards the edge of the spinning-top, you become increasingly disorientated, but the nearer you are to the centre, the more clear you become. This is analogous to inner work. Within us is our peaceful centre around which revolves the brilliant, playful and exciting drama of life.

When we first come to inner work we are spinning around on the edge of the top. As we grow in awareness and insight, our orientation becomes finer.

Smaller matters disturb our equilibrium because, as we tune more finely to our centre, the slighter the dissonance, the stronger the disturbance. Eventually, there are only the tiny revolutions in the middle and, finally, we find ourselves in the last revolutions, which are slow, unimpassioned and un-dramatic.

As you deepen in the spiritual journey, into the middle of the spinning-top, you may find that little things disturb you disproportionately. Others find you difficult to get on with. You become harder to live with. But this is an encouraging sign. We have to journey in to the middle to the still point, the heart, beyond the opposites, beyond space and time, to the Higher Self that is always there. Authentic experience draws us inwards and calls us back to our centre.

· SURRENDER IN ACTION ·

The Taoist concept *wu-wei* translates as 'non-action', but it is not inactivity; it is action without self-interest – surrendered action.[6] An act that proceeds out of non-action is spontaneous, free, pure and devoid of motivation, desire or intention. Non-action is being in the moment, without interfering with the flow of life. In the state of *wu-wei*, we align ourselves with higher power and act out of emptiness.

Acting out of true emptiness can be spectacularly effective, as when an aikido master defeats an attacker. Or it can take place in more subtle ways:

'Are you aware of his right trapezius muscle?' It is the voice of an older man, himself a therapist. He is easily old enough to be my father. He has been coming to my workshops for sometime now and seems to delight in finding ways to try to undermine me. I am engaged in some hands-on bodywork surrounded by an attentive audience and the remark rankles and amuses me at the same time. Later on it is his turn to work. After three quarters of an hour I have exhausted my therapist's toolbox. He is slumped in the middle of the rest of the group, who are sitting in a close, concerned circle. It is obvious to me that nothing I can do will help him to access his feelings. Then it dawns on me that the more effort I put into doing, into trying to get him to let go, the stronger is his deep need to 'win' by undermining me. Although he is suffering in a genuine impasse, caught in powerful feelings of not being loved as a child, he would rather that I was shown up and seen as ineffective than release his feelings.

This is the wall I have reached and I relax. If there is nothing I can 'do' then I won't 'do' anything. So I wait... and I wait... and I find I am experiencing a deep kinship with this man. I know that I have to act out of real love and, before I know it, I am sitting cross-legged inside the group circle rocking this big elderly man who is curled up in my lap crying like a child.

Non-action is not forcing, but flowing and allowing yourself to become one with the energy of the universe. The small self maintains you in proud self-containment, but when you act against the true nature of things you are truly lost. When you decide to fight, you separate yourself from your wholeness so that you cannot possibly win. The very moment you try to dominate, you are defeated.

Wu-wei is the outcome of surrendering all sense of a personal 'I'. Actions still happen, but there is no 'doer'. The *Tao Te Ching* states:

In the pursuit of learning, every day something is acquired
[as regards our efforts and expectations].
In the pursuit of the Tao, every day something is dropped
[as regards our business and desires].
Less and less is done
Until non-action is achieved.
When nothing is done, nothing is left undone.
The world is ruled by letting things take their course.
It cannot be ruled by interfering.[7]

· SYNCHRONICITY ·

Synchronicity describes how seemingly separate events are significantly connected. As we ally ourselves with unity and surrender – the process of awakening to the Divine – we increasingly notice the oneness of all things. Nothing should be assumed to be meaningless or insignificant, because everything is connected and divine.

The book that introduced us to Zen, which we happened to reach for from a friend's bookshelf, the dream that set us thinking about something new and changed our life direction, the missed appointment that led us to an unexpected meeting with the person who first introduced us to inner work – all of these are examples of synchronicity.

> [Synchronicity] takes the coincidence of events in space and time as meaning something more then mere chance, namely, a peculiar interdependence of objective events among themselves as well as with the subjective (psychic) states of the observer or observers.[8]

This is Jung's classic explanation. Contemporary writers summarize synchronicity as meaningful, and mysterious, coincidence. But it is much more than either of these definitions suggest. It is the view of the spiritual path through the window of space and time. It is how events in the temporal world affect our spiritual emergence. The more we consider synchronicity as it manifests in dreams, chance events, significant people, intuition and premonition, the more we see that it simply describes the nature of the spiritual path. Synchronicity is an integral part of spiritual life, reflecting the relationship, the intelligence, and the natural order of our destinies.

We may think of the inner journey as a return to the historical impasses, which are the origin of our constriction and our lack of freedom. Or, we may think of it as the deepening into the present in which the experiences of the past are simply a layer, an imprinted level of our present experience. But, since time is not a consideration of the Divine, we may view our inner journey in a third way: whatever happens in the present moment is the perfect teaching of life. Then, synchronous events are a form of guidance that very commonly occurs to people who have chosen the spiritual path. The philosopher Goethe wrote:

> Until one is committed, there is hesitancy, the chance to draw back, always ineffectiveness. Concerning acts of initiative (and creation) there is one elementary truth the ignorance of which kills countless ideas and splendid plans: that the moment one definitely commits oneself then Providence moves too.
>
> All sorts of things occur to help one that would never otherwise have occurred. A whole stream of events issues from the decision, raising in one's favour all manner of unforeseen incidents and meetings and material assistance, which no one could have dreamt would come their way.

Whatever you can do, or dream you can, begin it. Boldness has genius, power and magic in it. Begin it now.[9]

Make everything significant, consider nothing to be meaningless coincidence, notice everything and use it all, let it all in, learn to listen, learn to hear the world and what it is saying to you, whether in precognitive dreaming...

I had a dream of three long, parallel ditches in the ground. The dream puzzled me. I could make no sense of it at all. Shortly afterwards I came across the same three ditches in a field. They turned out to be excavations for the foundations of the building where I would begin my inner journey.

... or meaningful occurrence...

I was leading a trust exercise. Half a dozen people were standing in a circle around a woman who was telling me how she had always been afraid to trust. This was going to be hard but I was sure it would work for her. 'This is safe', I said. She began to lean towards the group participants, who gently resisted the slight fall and guided her around the circle. Suddenly, she fell through the middle of two participants and straight onto the ground! She was unhurt, but not only that, she was elated, because in facing her inability to trust – and the very worst happening – she was released from her fear.

... or pure, poetic synchronicity:

It was Sarah's birthday. I was going to bed when she called to me to stay and share a bottle of wine with her and a few friends. She broke the cork trying to open the bottle so that the cork was left half in. In her struggle to extract the cork she broke the handle of the corkscrew so that the metal screw remained stuck in the cork. We all took turns to push or pull the cork. I asked Sarah about her birth. 'I was a breech birth', she said. 'I got stuck and they couldn't get me out'. I felt her deep anxiety and tension as she described her birth experience. 'You have to go', I told her, 'then we will be able to open the bottle'. She didn't understand, but as soon as she left the room the cork popped out of the bottle.

·The Play of Consciousness·

You might say that to be truly realized you have to get to the point where you are not seeking anymore. So that you begin to think, 'Well, I will now be a nonseeker.

Alan Watts

We are inclined to take ourselves too seriously. On some occasions, we feel overly important and, on others, we feel totally insignificant. How can we find the balance between these two extremes?

When we feel important for what we do and for what we have, we are overly concerned with the material world of ambition and acquisition. Our emotional well-being seems to depend entirely on our outer worldly success. But we confuse the gift-wrap for the gift. What makes us important and unique is what is at our core, what we are in the spaces between breaths, and the essence of truth, which lies deep within the Self.

When we confuse the posturings of the small self with the reality of the Self, we serve the ego and become self-important and ridiculous. Consider the role of the comedian, the contemporary equivalent of the court-jester – the wise fool. A good comedian can make us laugh at ourselves by persuading, or reminding, us of the absurdity of life. He lays psychological traps and finally snares us. We laugh or cry, as we release the tensions of seriousness and self-importance. This is the skill of the comedian and the art of wise foolishness.

We must deeply accept the inevitable aspects of life – life and death, good and evil, success and failure – and open up and learn from them. Surrendering our sense of personal power and control is one of the most difficult challenges in the spiritual journey.

You must 'dance' with life, but if your cheek is too tightly up against life, you might be out of relationship with it altogether. Too close or too far – either disturbs the delicate boundary, which enables true meeting. Withdraw when you need to, meet when you need to – let your relationship with life be like the rhythmic beat of your heart.

> … let the winds of the heavens dance between you…
> And stand together yet not too near together:
> For the pillars of the temple stand apart,
> And the oak tree and the cypress grow not in each other's shadow.[10]

· BRILLIANT DISGUISE ·

Live in the world, but do not get lost in it or consumed by it. You are divine – that is your reality. No effort is required – simply realization. You realize your divinity when you surrender to the Self. The Self is always within, always perfect in your heart, both faceless and beyond appearance and, simultaneously, all faces and all appearances. You have adopted a brilliant disguise – it is your 'me-ness', your small self, and this must be surrendered to the unconscious forces of the Divine for transformation. Sylvia Brinton Perera writes:

> We are forced to offer what we hold dear, what we have paid much to gain. And we cannot even know that the loss will be recompensed in the ways that we desire. The sacrifice may change the balance of energy somewhere in the over-all psychic system where we did not even want a change. All that we can know is that finding renewal and connection… will involve breaking up the old pattern, the death of a gestalt we were comfortable with on some level, the death of a seemingly whole identity.[11]

When we understand that we are in disguise we can live life less seriously and dramatically – in the light of wisdom and truth. We can be serious about life in a different way now that we are aware of the profundity of existence. We are able to play because Divine play is closer to the essence of life than seriousness and self-importance. We can participate in the world in the deep knowledge that its endless, changing appearance is all a chimera. In the last days of his life Aldous Huxley wrote:

> The world is an illusion, but it is an illusion that we must take seriously… We must not live thoughtlessly, taking our illusion for the complete reality… We must not attempt to live outside the world, which is given us, but we must somehow learn how to transform it and transfigure it… One must find a way of being in the world while not being of it.[12]

We need not become lost in life. We have the perspective that allows us to participate totally. Eternal consciousness plays in the world and invites us to join in life's roles and dramas – the fabulous deception – in our brilliant disguise.

· SELF-IMPORTANCE ·

Sometimes we meet people who push us to the limits of our patience, tolerance and understanding. Their actions seem to pursue us and we dearly wish that they were not in our lives. Ironically, these people show us where we are losing our energy as they reflect back to us our inner problems. This can help us to recognize the problems and do something about them. We often receive more help and guidance from our enemies than from our friends, but our self-glorification prevents us from recognizing and using that help. It is helpful to depersonalize these people by reflecting on the fact that if it were not them, it would be somebody else. Our projection onto them as the cause of our problems is usually so overwhelming that we are tremendously resistant to even admitting to the problem they are helping to illuminate. Carlos Castaneda's Don Juan said:

> Self-importance is our greatest enemy... what weakens us is feeling offended by the deeds and misdeeds of our fellow men. Our self-importance requires that we spend most of our lives offended by someone.[13]

The victim inside us holds on to the memory of real or imagined affronts. We create inner scenarios of revenge and retribution out of the, usually unconscious, anger that we nurture against the people who have slighted us. But if we see how much of our energy is going into holding onto anger and revenge, we find out that it is not them, but us, who is paying the price and the price is usually a high one. The energy that our self-importance invests in revenge saps our strength and depletes us more than we appreciate.

In modern movies and novels the perennial themes are romance, comedy and revenge – and the theme of revenge is extremely popular. The actors Clint Eastwood and Charles Bronson have built their careers on it, as have their successors, Bruce Willis, Arnold Schwarzenegger and a succession of others. These actors are very often typecast as vengeful characters, because we the audience have become addicted to revenge, particularly when it is justified. We want to find a valid reason for giving the guy back 'what he deserves', which justifies our anger and hate, and exonerates us. Our self-importance requires offence, so that we can be justified in the role of the victim who gets his own back. One of the best examples is Sam Peckinpah's war movie *Cross of Iron*. In the final scene, a senior officer who has given an order to fire on his own men, becomes trapped in a trench with the corporal who led the men who were fired on. The corporal aims his machine gun at the cringing officer and there is a lull in the action – a frozen moment – and we are given the chance to imagine ourselves in the corporal's shoes with our finger on the trigger. Would we shoot? When we are at the mercy of uncontrolled emotion, it is we ourselves who are overwhelmed. Don Juan again:

> To act in anger, without control and discipline, to have no forbearance, is to be defeated.[14]

A moment of all-consuming passion, the heady mixture of justification and righteousness, strong emotion and will, may prove hard to resist. But if we place ourselves out of the separate, separating, divisive ego then we can see that anything we do to our enemy, we do to ourselves, and anything our enemy does to us, he does to himself.

Our self-importance demands power over other people. But when we surrender our power to the Higher Self, we relinquish the desire to have power over others. We then say, 'Not my will, but Thy will be done'.

·GOALLESS-NESS·

We spend a considerable amount of the present in an imagined future. Our thoughts race ahead and we project our bodies forward in time. Rarely are our thoughts and our awareness focused on the present. We can learn a lot about how to focus from walking meditation – particularly slow walking meditation. Thich Nhat Hanh says:

> Walking meditation is really to enjoy the walking – walking not in order to arrive, but just to walk. The purpose is to be in the present moment and aware of our breathing and our walking, to enjoy each step... We can do it only if we do not think of the future or the past, if we know that life can only be found in the present moment.[15]

End gaining is a key idea in the Alexander Technique. It describes how we lose touch with ourselves in our efforts to reach our goals. When we focus on a goal, we become obsessed with achieving it and distracted from the steps we need to take to reach it. The Alexander teacher asks you to sit down in, and then get up from, a chair. To your astonishment you find that you are not mentally and physically present as you perform these movements.

When was the last time you remember sitting down onto a chair? How do you do it? Rather than have your thoughts race ahead to the future, bring your attention to the process of sitting. What is the process that takes place between your intention to sit and your carrying it out? When you bring close attention to these details of your behaviour, you become more aware and more present because you are less focused on the goal of your actions.

Goalless-ness describes the journey, not the destination. When we open to life as a process, we see that our whole life is 'a becoming' that is never ending. Conversely, if our model of life is a series of staccato incidents with pauses, we perceive life as events and non-events and we create dissatisfaction and boredom. When we live life as a process there is no end that we are trying to gain, no goal that we are trying to reach. Striving for goals levies a high cost on being, presence, and the enjoyment of life. How often do we struggle to reach a goal and, in reaching it, lose everything else? Living our life as a process, without having to reach a goal, requires us being present and finding all that we need in the present. We need the humility to not know and the wisdom to see that we are always beginning – in wise innocence. Thomas Merton wrote:

> Those who think they 'know' from the beginning never, in fact, come to know anything... We do not want to be beginners. But let us be convinced of the fact that we will never be anything else but beginners, all our life.[16]

Spiritual practice is the alchemy of ordinary life: we practise in the moment to actualize the Eternal. Truth is the goal *and* the practice, so there is nothing to gain, nothing to lose and nothing to achieve. In the Buddha's *Diamond Sutra*, this is true of the highest spiritual achievement:

> What did I gain from full and perfect Enlightenment? Nothing whatever.[17]

Synchronicity, goalless-ness, and wu-wei are all aspects of surrender. Surrendering the past and the future presents us with the moment, surrendering self-motivated action offers us the universe, surrendering our goals yields everything. The spiritual way is non-acquisitive, because there is nothing for us to hoard. Everything we desired, lost, or willed was inside us all along. As we reach the centre of the spinning-top, we become centred in the Self and deeply empowered – and where we find ourselves is ordinary and strangely familiar. From *The Upanishads*:

> When the sun has set, and the moon has set, and the fire is gone out, and the sound hushed, what is then the light of man?
> The Self indeed is his light; for having the Self alone as his light, man sits, moves about, does his work, and returns.
> Who is that Self?
> He who is within the heart, surrounded by the senses, the person of light...

EXPANSION

Man as he now is has ceased to be the All. But when he ceases to be an
individual, he raises himself again and penetrates the whole world. **Plotinus**

As we pass through the middle stages of the spiritual journey, we need to look for authority and wisdom *inside* ourselves. We have reached a level of spiritual maturation and, if we continue to refer outside ourselves, we will get stuck in outward dependence and be unable to go any farther. We are entering a period of expansion. Our habitual way of handling fear, pain or sorrow is to contract, which is a function of our character defences. True expansion lessens our character, which contains and defends the small self. This is a time of new beginnings, as we grieve at the death of the old self. Now we must go beyond our separate selves to fulfil our Divine potential.

In this stage we consider personal and spiritual empowerment, how we project authority, the alchemy of emotions, relationships as a vehicle for spiritual growth, the generous heart, inner wisdom and Divine longing.

·EXPANSION AND EMPOWERMENT·

We have learned to fear our potential and this alienates us from our true selves. We collude with others by denying our personal power, so that we do not become too conspicuous. We disempower others, and ourselves, verbally, physically, and mentally.

Consider your models of power and what they teach you. Most often our models of power are based on some form of domination. We desire to have power 'over' other people, but personal power is not power 'over' others. It is being truly who we are.

Ask yourself, 'How do I disempower myself?' and 'What do I get out of doing it?' Since we are not who we think we are, we have to radically re-orientate ourselves. We have a deep responsibility to be all that we can be, to be truly ourselves. Ironically, we hide the many magnificent qualities, which empower us. All along we have been afraid of our own brightness.

Our deepest fear is not that we are inadequate.
Our deepest fear is that we are powerful beyond measure.
It is our light, not our darkness, that most frightens us.
We ask ourselves, 'Who am I to be brilliant, gorgeous, talented, fabulous?'
Actually, who are you not to be?
You are a child of God.
Your playing small doesn't serve the world.
There's nothing enlightened about shrinking
So that other people won't feel insecure around you.
We are all meant to shine as children do.
We are born to make manifest the glory of God that is within us.
It's not just in some of us; it's in everyone.
And as we let our light shine,
We unconsciously give other people permission to do the same.
As we are liberated from our own fear,
Our presence automatically liberates others.[1]

· EXPANDING YOUR CONSCIOUSNESS ·

Our small selves identify with negativity and contraction. If we redirect even a little of the energy that we use to hold on to fear, anger and pain, we can experience an expansive change.

When we expand our energy, we become sensitive to the energetic states of others. We know how close we want to be to someone and where our boundaries are. When we fully occupy the energy field that surrounds us, others tend to be more sensitive towards us.

Where does our consciousness finish and everything else begin? Where is the boundary between inner and outer? Our complex minds anticipate events; our expectations delineate our experience. Any model that shapes our consciousness limits our reality, because consciousness has no limits. From within expanded consciousness we witness transcendent realities.

The inside information is that yourself as 'just little me' who 'came into this world' and lives temporarily in a bag of skin is a hoax and a fake. The fact is that because no one thing or feature of this universe is separable from the whole, the only real You, or Self, is the whole...

Alan Watts

I was not prepared for what happened. I was standing in the middle of a busy city high street on Monday morning. I had returned from a ten-day meditation retreat the night before. So the hustle and bustle of the city felt fresh and new. I stood watching the people move in and out and around each other, running and talking, avoiding and dawdling, anxious and self-assured. It was all so rich, like some marvellous, vivid painting. Each individual or group of characters came alive as I focused my attention on them. Then, quite suddenly, it all changed. The street, the shop windows, the trees, the traffic and the people all merged into a single whole; they appeared to be an indistinguishable unity. The people were no longer haphazardly or carelessly related. It was as if there was a divine choreography in which they all participated, moving around each other in agreed steps like some wonderful, prescribed sequence that mirrored their relationships to each other and to the mystical whole of which they were each a part. I gazed in awe and wonder for some seconds, until it all melted away and there was just the busy city high street once more.

Individual consciousness flows into unified Consciousness and only our personal constraints limit the scope of our awareness. We are connected to each other and to all things. Yet, in the West, we are conditioned to perceive ourselves as separate and isolated. When we restrict our consciousness, we deny ourselves the possibility of experiencing the transcendent. How we expand or limit our consciousness defines our experience. Karlfried Graf Durckheim wrote:

Expanding consciousness is one of the most important aspects of the Way of initiation...The vital thing on the Way of initiation is to avoid regressing, and to progress to that 'subjective' consciousness in which all the earlier stages, and particularly rational consciousness, are absorbed and transcended in a broadened consciousness.[2]

·Macrocosm and Minutiae·

In our enthusiasm for self-enquiry, we easily become obsessed with the minutiae of our lives. We give attention to the trivia and avoid the important issues. We require a sense of proportion. However sincerely we seek, the search will never be successful while we search in the wrong place.

There is a crazy wisdom story from the Sufi tradition about Mullah Nasrudin. Coming home late one night the Mullah dropped his front door key. As he was searching for the key on his hands and knees under a street lamp, a friend walked by and asked what he was doing.

'I am looking for my front-door key', explained the Mullah.
'Where did you lose it?' asked his friend.
'Over there', said the Mullah, gesturing towards a dark area in front of his house.
'So why are you searching here?' asked his perplexed friend.
'Because this is where the light is', explained the Mullah.

When I was in my twenties, I was obsessed with the small details of my personality and my behaviour. I would analyse and criticize myself minutely and work it up into a big drama. Even a relatively minor event would leave me questioning why I had a certain character fault. I was obsessed with the impact of my early life and how it had affected me. I sought the answers to all my problems in the past.

In our youth we focus on the big picture. We immerse ourselves in thoughts towards the macrocosm and direct our souls out. This is the outward reflection of our inward self-obsession. Our obsession with self at this stage is so overwhelming that we project it onto the macrocosm. As we mature into middle years, our focus changes and we become less concerned with the details of life as our souls turn inward and we seek the macrocosm within.

·Projecting Authority·

No person or teaching can replace our inner authority, although we may use either as a means to discover it. But when we defer to an outer authority over our own, we become the oppressors of ourselves. Whether it is a religion, a guru, a therapist, or a friend, do not substitute your inner knowing for any other.

A Zen master and his disciple were walking down a muddy road in heavy rain. Rounding a bend in the road they came upon a lovely young woman in a beautiful silk kimono and sash, standing helplessly at the edge of a fast-flowing stream. The master lifted her in his arms and carried her across. The monks continued on their way in silence.

Eventually, unable to contain himself any longer, the disciple said, 'We monks are forbidden to touch females – especially young and lovely ones. It is dangerous. Why did you do that?'

'I left the girl back there,' replied the master, 'Are you still carrying her?'

Like the Zen master in the story, we can do what is necessary and let go, or, like the disciple, we can get caught in the details and miss the deeper teaching. The expansive mind deepens into the essence of the teaching, which is always aimed at enlightenment.

Inner wisdom informs enlightened action; enlightened action is acting without attachment. Sri Nisargadatta Maharaj suggests complete surrender:

Suffering is due entirely to clinging or resisting. It is a sign of our unwillingness to move on, to flow with life... The essence of saintliness is total acceptance of the present moment, harmony with things as they happen. A saint does not want things to be different from what they are... He is friendly with the inevitable and therefore does not suffer. ... If he can, he does what is needful to restore the lost balance – or he lets things take their course. [3]

· EMOTIONAL ALCHEMY ·

Emotional energy can change our consciousness and fuel our expansion. In order to do this we have to make a qualitative leap. We take the raw energy of emotion and transmute it into higher energy. Physically, the movement is from the lower energy centres to the higher ones. Energy should flow throughout the body. When the flow is constrained, we may experience unbearable emotion.

Two young men were openly antagonizing each other on the workshop. They had been competing for the same young woman and they wanted to 'work'. Their agenda was to slug it out and rage at each other in front of her with a heap of cushions between them. Clearly, each hoped that this enactment of primitive conflict would result in the victor getting the girl. They were puffing out their chests and breathing heavily in preparation for the struggle that was to come. Just as they were about to engage with each other, the group leader asked them to wait and said, 'Could you be bigger than this?'

They looked at him like hunters, asked to give up their kill. Blind emotion and aggression were so strong in them that it had to find release somehow.

They looked at each other in mutual recognition and began to glow and pulsate with a different kind of energy – the energy of reconciliation. We sat around them feeling these powerful waves of energy. It was transformation in process. Finally, they both moved towards each other and embraced over the cushions.

This is our choice: to dissipate our emotional energy or to transform it through emotional alchemy.

Do you remember the scene at the end of the film *One Flew Over the Cuckoo's Nest* when the Indian nicknamed 'Chief' throws the control panel through the window in the tub-room and escapes? He had spent years in psychiatric prison in a state of resignation and passivity. The oppressive authorities believed that he was deaf and dumb. What fuelled his escape? It was the strong feelings aroused in him by the raw, uninhibited hero, McMurphy (played by Jack Nicholson). In the end McMurphy faces a living death, while Chief realizes McMurphy's vision and liberates himself. The powerful emotional connection with McMurphy led to his expansion.

We should never forget that we are already conscious. We are spiritually realized beings waiting to return to ourselves. When our passion, energy and vitality have built up to bursting point through fear, anger, sorrow or

I found the world rapt in an inexpressible glory with its waves of joy and beauty bursting and breaking on all sides. The thick cloud of sorrow that lay on my heart in many folds was pierced through and through by the light of the world, which was everywhere radiant. There was nothing and no one whom I did not love at that moment.

Rabindranath Tagore

101

pain, the opportunity has arisen for us to open and expand. We should always be ready and open to that opportunity. We are always more than we think we are. Karlfried Graf Durckheim wrote:

> ... what does 'open' mean? It means open *in consciousness*, or better, *as* consciousness. We must become sufficiently transparent for Being to manifest in us as Life, consciously sensed, responsibly accepted, and pouring itself out into the world. To make this possible, our consciousness must change... [4]

•LIFE AS POETRY, LIFE AS PROSE•

Most of us live life sequentially, practically, and rationally and quell the spontaneous, irrational, and artistic forces within. We live our lives as prose, rather than poetry.

When we live our lives as poetry, we find that the small self and its primary instrument, the mind, become less important. Living life as poetry rounds off our corners, opens us to the natural flow, and vivifies the beauty of life. We are less concerned with reasons and divisions, and the Self is at once the centre and the outer reaches of our consciousness. Poetry awakens us to expansive experience, bridges the worlds of inner and outer, and connects us to the whole of Life.

> [Poetry is]... a vocabulary in the form not of words but of acts and adventures, which connotes something transcendent of the action here, so that you always feel in accord with the universal being.[5]

As poetry, the moment is infinite; as prose, it is a fraction of a minute. As prose, life is play or work, morning or evening, this or that; as poetry, life simply is. Prose presses on to a goal; poetry remains in the present.

Living life as poetry reminds us of sacred dance: the dance of Shiva conjuring the universe, dancing to the rhythm of eternity. When the individual heart beats in unison with the cosmic heartbeat there is only one single Consciousness. The dancer becomes one with the dance. Jesus expressed this idea in the *Gnostic Gospels*:

To the Universe belongs the dancer. He who does not dance does not know what happens. Now if you follow my dance, see yourself in Me who am speaking... You who dance, consider what I do, for yours is this passion of Man which I am to suffer.[6]

The poem, or the dance, offers a threshold through which we may mediate between our humanness and our divinity, between individuality and unity, between time and eternity.

When we dance or express ourselves through poetry, we evoke the gods and their mythological worlds. We become elemental forces, forces of nature, and so become closer to nature. We are 'held' within the interplay of forces far more powerful than our individual separateness will allow. Gods and goddesses, myths and archetypes, are reflections of the Self.

·EXPANSION AND RELATIONSHIPS·

Personal relationships are a precious opportunity for spiritual growth and expansion. The unity of two consciousnesses can enable each partner to transcend their small selves, because the love that we feel for another human being connects us to divine love. The poet Rilke wrote:

For one human being to love another: that is perhaps the most difficult of all our tasks, the ultimate, the last test and proof, the work for which all the other work is but preparation.[7]

When only one partner in a relationship sets out on the spiritual journey, the threat is extreme. The other is almost forced into the growth process and may be stubborn and reactive as a result. Many couples break up over this issue, only to find that some time later the one who 'refused' to embark on the inner journey decides to do so after a 'cooling off' period, by which time the relationship is past saving. In the meantime, they have managed to integrate the aspect of themselves that their partner was living out by following his or her own spiritual journey.

When a couple first meet, there is a rigorous process of 'vetting' on behalf of the unconscious to establish the other's suitability as a partner. The deep criteria for a match concern growth and the journey to wholeness. We are looking for a partner who will help us to face ourselves through a process of projection and the play of polarities.

A suitable partner represents all that we fundamentally disown in ourselves and we represent this for our partner too. The danger is that this enables us to justify our life statements, and carry on leading our familiar lives and following our habitual patterns. The alternative is to seize the opportunity to work through and re-own the projected parts of us, integrate our disowned polarities and work towards personal wholeness.

The Greek myth of Psyche and Eros describes the path of relationship. Psyche is the human longing for the Divine and Eros is the god seeking his humanity. Thus this myth symbolizes the relationship of the human and the divine. We are guided to the inner marriage through the trials of projection, mistrust, abandonment, and fear. The spiritual journey of Psyche tells how the heart expands and learns to love.

The inner marriage is the celebration of our wholeness. It signifies the transcendence of the opposites, the reconciling of male and female within, and the integration of our spiritual nature in our consciousness.

·THE GENEROUS HEART·

A generous heart is a reflection of the abundance of the universe. Receiving should be a gracious and humble act, because in true receiving there is also giving. True giving is a complete act with no investment in the outcome.

Generosity can take many forms. An open heart is a generous heart and in openness there is transparency and honesty. Generosity is sometimes a challenge. For example, telling someone what we really think and feel may be uncomfortable; we might rock the boat, but the generous heart can meet the challenge.

Our openness and honesty invite the other to open and expand, to lessen their attachment to collusive or manipulative relationship. Our giving invites the other to give.

Sometimes this experience is positive and beautiful. At other times we are asked to say the 'un-sayable' – and that might be just what is needed. When we are on the receiving end we can feel the sharp edges. When under attack, the ego can react by producing the inflated self.

Many years ago I co-led a workshop with a German psychodrama therapist. When it was over, my co-leader insisted on having a mutual feedback session. She said, 'I have to tell you that you looked like the caricature of a therapist. When anybody spoke you nodded vigorously and you just kept nodding. You looked like one of those dogs on the back shelf of a car.'

Now the small 'me' felt unfairly criticized and defensive, while my expansive self was receptive to what she said. My expansive self knew she was right. I had been working with a therapist who would nod vigorously – it was part of her 'style'. I admired the way she did this because it communicated warmth and enthusiastic attention to me. In contrast to her, my perception of myself was that I had an unfeeling façade. Partly unconsciously, I had been trying out her style, to see if I could improve on my presentation. But it was inauthentic, it was not 'me'. Listening to my co-leader's feedback the expansive part of me was saying, 'OK, she's right, I can take that,' and the reactive, contracted part of me was saying, 'Who are you to say these things to me!'. And that created the inflated, puffed-up me. The expansive part was able to hear what she was saying, while my inflated self was unable to get past my defences.

·HIJACKING THE SPIRITUAL·

On a Theravadin Buddhist meditation retreat I attended, one of the rules was that we were not allowed to write. About three days into the retreat I was experiencing such tremendous insights that I could no longer resist writing them down. Over the remaining days of the retreat, I surreptitiously recorded my inner experiences and produced a precious pile of written sheets. On my return home I placed the sheets reverently on my desk in anticipation of the inspiration I expected to receive from them. However, I found none of the great spiritual insights I had expected, but rather plain and uninspired thoughts.

The small self attempts to use spiritual attainment for its own ends and it tries to identify with the Self. The ego inflates by identifying with something greater than itself. The results are moral superiority, becoming dictatorial and patronizing, the loss of genuineness, and vulnerability. The spirit does shine through you as you deepen into the Higher Self; but any attempts to hijack the qualities of the spirit for ego ends – whether subtle or overt – are thwarted.

In Wu Ch'eng-en's classic story, *Monkey*, Buddha proposed a wager.

Buddha promised Monkey the throne of the Jade Emperor (from whom all beings have their ultimate origin) if he could jump off the palm of his right hand. If he failed he would have to leave heaven and return to earth for many *kalpas* (a single *kalpa* numbers more than 4 million human years). Monkey considered this a very easy bet to win. Buddha stretched out his right hand and Monkey took his leap.

He arrived at five pink pillars. He thought he was at the end of the world and considered the throne his. Before he returned he decided to leave some evidence of his grand leap, in case Buddha contested the claim. He wrote at the base of the central pillar, 'The Great Sage Equal to Heaven reached this place,' then, as a mark of disrespect, he urinated at the base of the first pillar and somersaulted back.

Standing on Buddha's palm he demanded his throne. But Buddha declared that he had been there all the time. Monkey corrected Buddha and offered to take him to the flesh-coloured pillars to show him the proof.

'No need for that,' said Buddha. 'Just look down.'

Monkey peered down with his fiery eyes and at the base of Buddha's middle finger he saw written, 'The Great Sage Equal to Heaven reached this place,' and at the fork of the thumb and the first finger he saw a tiny puddle of stinking, yellowish liquid.

The Self is All. It can never be defeated, contained or transcended. Our small self may attempt to outdo the spiritual in futile acts of self-aggrandizement but it never succeeds.

The simplicity of the spiritual path evades the rational, complex mind. Spiritual seeking is sometimes confused with material acquisition, which it does not resemble in the slightest. The jewel is already in our own hearts. As one spiritual master once advised a disciple, 'Expect nothing, seek nothing, just live'.[8]

·Grief for the Old Self·

As we work, gently but persistently, at releasing our attachment to the self, we go through a significant transformation. One of the signs that this transformation is happening is feeling grief with no obvious cause. The cause turns out to be very obvious, however, when we notice that who we were and how we lived our life is now passing away. We are feeling grief at the death of the old self.

You need to feel this grief, for it empowers you to go on. Grief is a sign that your attachment to the self is finally lessening. It is also an integral part of your journey. You are dying to your contracted identity and facing the unknown – you are growing and expanding.

This is the time for working through your regrets – 'what-ifs' and 'if-onlys'. When someone close to you dies, you think of the things you wished you had told them and the things you wished you had done together. Now you must address the same issues in relation to your old self.

You need to review your history of pain and hurt, anger and sorrow, need and fulfilment, tranquillity and joy, longing and satisfaction. How have you lived your life? How deeply? How fully? Has your experience of life opened your heart or closed it? Did you succumb to bitterness, sadness or regret? Were you a willing student of life? Did your spirit fly?

The death of the separate self brings up the fear of extinction, yet it is the fading of the self that propels you into true existence. Find a way to honour the old self for whom you are grieving. Find a way to lay regrets to rest. Acknowledge your victories and failures, express and ritualize what remains, and allow all of your feelings.

·Inner Wisdom of the Self·

Inner wisdom is simple and always available. All we have to do is learn to ask and listen. We connect with our inner wisdom in just the same way as we hold a conversation.

We might ask, 'What do I need to know now?' and, listening, we may hear the answer, 'You are doing just fine,' and this may be the reassurance we need. We might ask, 'What do I need to know about my family?' and, listening, we may hear the answer, 'Be more present so you can open your heart,' and this may be the guidance we need. We might ask, 'How can I make more money?' and, listening, we may hear the answer, 'You have all you need'.

If any of you lacks wisdom, he should ask God who gives generously to all without finding fault, and it will be given to him.[9]

Hearing the answer clearly is obviously vital. This is easier when we are not invested in the answer coming out a particular way. When we are invested in the outcome of the question, we may inhibit the clarity of the answer. When this happens we think, either, that our inner wisdom has dried up, or, that the answer is not clear. Therefore, it is helpful to empty yourself of expectations before you ask your question and be as neutral as you can towards the potential answer, so you can at least hear what it is. The answer always comes; simply be available to hear it.

Genuine guidance is spontaneous and immediate. You may only get the very next step, not the detailed plan for the future that your mind desires. But when the time is right, you will receive guidance about the next step. Do not make the mistake of asking your wisdom for guidance and then ignoring it. Never invalidate the guidance that you receive. Always respond to it, feel grateful for it and honour it.

Wisdom differs from knowledge: knowledge is acquired, whereas wisdom is inherent. Knowledge is of no use whatsoever on the spiritual path. It has no spiritual importance in itself; it is simply an acquisition. Wisdom, on the other hand, is our greatest treasure and an inner gift you discover in your Eternal Heart. Alan Watts wrote:

The Knower
The central Self
is not born and
Does not die.

It is not produced from anything
And produces nothing apart from itself.
It is unborn, eternal, enduring, primordial.

It is not slain when the body is slain.
If the slayer thinks he slays
Or the slain thinks he is slain
Neither understands.
It neither slays nor can be slain.

Smaller than the small
Greater than the great
It is the self in the heart of all being.[10]

·DIVINE LONGING·

Our deep desire to return to our original nature, to realize the true Self, is known as divine longing. Divine longing is our spiritual motivation and, inherent in it, is our deepest sense of belonging. Sometimes the sense of belonging 'elsewhere' turns us away from the world. Often the human realm seems so ugly and terrible, insensitive and unenlightened — a kind of hell.

Yet here also is the heaven we seek — where else could it be? It is here in this world that we have to realize the Self and actualize the Divine through the spiritual journey. Both heaven and hell are a continuum of transformation, and we are capable of either. When we reject hell, we reject heaven too. When we turn away from the ugly face of humanity, we turn away also from the glorious face of the Divine. We have to be careful that we do not exploit divine longing to divert us towards a spiritual mirage, where we wish only to see the beautiful. Salvation cannot be based on a lie.

Passion is a powerful force for realization when it can be released from objects of desire. Sometimes we can have an experience that liberates us from our normal constraints so that we experience passion as a subjective state, not as the driving hunger behind the desire for an outer object or another person. A moment can be all it takes to release us:

The pebbles were shining magically under the little stream of gurgling water.
Brilliant bubbles filled with sunlight exploded all over the surface of the water.
It was all so beautiful and transcendent, full of enchantment. I leant closer

and, accidentally, immersed my face in the moving water. As I inhaled I breathed in water inadvertently. I panicked. The primal fear of death surged through me. I leapt up, crying like a newborn baby. I was totally open. My teacher laughed insanely and paddled water into my face with his hands as I wept. When the crying stopped, I stood still for a long time. The air around me was filled with being, with God. Miracles took place all around me. Off to my right, a bonfire appeared on the water, just beyond my physical vision. A band of incredible beings – elves, fairies, dwarves, animals – clothed in their finery, filed into the glade behind me playing drums, cymbals, flutes, shaking bells and carrying leafy boughs and armfuls of flowers. Somehow I 'saw' all of this without turning round. When they had finished playing, we wandered off. In a field the scene of a medieval battle was played out before me, from the first thunderous charge to the silent stillness of the fallen slain. Accidentally, I stepped in a cowpat and created the most beautiful pattern of shape, texture and colour in which I saw God. God in a cowpat seemed like a cosmic joke. We laughed ecstatically. I saw the Divine everywhere. I walked in the sunlight through the fields, over the gates, among the trees, and everywhere everything was sacred, beautiful, blissful and blessed. Gratitude welled up in my heart and surged through me. I became heart, I became devotion and through my tears I was filled with passion and love for the whole of life.

Passion takes us to our 'edge', the brink of the unknown; it is a feeling of the soul. If we take the the longing and the desire we experience when falling in love, and broaden its focus, we can live with the same intensity of passion for existence. The mystic poet Rumi recognized and celebrated the deep longing of the human heart for the Divine. In his poetry the Divine becomes his Lover and his Beloved.

> I did not know the bliss that was so near to me, for my love was not yet awake. But now, my Lover has made known to me the meaning of the note that struck my ear: Now, my good fortune is come... Behold! How great is my good fortune! I have received the unending caress of my Beloved! [11]

The depth and intensity of our longing for the Eternal can bring about a meeting with the Divine. Ramakrishna said:

It is said if a man can weep for God one day and one night, he sees Him.[12]

Expansion breaks down the barriers between self and other so that the experience of the other can be felt, as if it were our very own.

> I had been living in a Soto Zen monastery for some time. The silence, the peace and the spiritual focus had begun to sharpen me up, so that when I was engaged in an activity, I was extremely present. I was rubbing down a small, wooden trolley, which had been donated to the monastery kitchen. Long ago it had been painted with thick white gloss paint and the Chief Cook wanted it rubbed down to the original wood. As I rubbed, I felt the layers of my conditioning, my own veneer and covering, being rubbed away. In the deep silence and contemplative atmosphere of the monastery there was an intimacy of unimaginable closeness. I had heard about a friend's mother: her house had burnt down and the old lady had lost a lifetime of irreplaceable belongings. Rubbing the wood, I began to feel her in my heart and, clutching the sandpaper tightly in my hand, I wept for her. It was not sentimental in any way and I was not identifying with her – I was really weeping for her and for her distress. Her sorrow and her grief were my own.

ONENESS WITH THE SELF

The knower and the known are one. Simple people imagine that they should see God as if He stood there and they here. This is not so. God and I, we are one in knowledge.

Meister Eckhart

The waves of expansion spiral out of the yielding emptiness of our new consciousness. They refer us inwards to our centre and closer to the meeting with the Self that brings about inner unity. For this to happen the unknown must be faced and the things of the individual self finally surrendered. We undergo a dark night of the soul – the crossing of the threshold of the unconscious to wholeness. The whole person is all and everything; the whole person is the Self.

In this stage we describe the Axis Mundi – the Self as the centre of the world, the surrender of the self, the dark night of the soul, the condition of no-seeking and being at OM. We have the unique opportunity to live our life and the responsibility to be ourselves. Only when we are truly ourselves can we be totally alone; only when we can be totally alone are we connected to the Whole. As we rise to the best in ourselves, we realize the 'I am' of existence.

·YOU ARE THE CENTRE OF THE WORLD·

Deep inside you is your still centre. The outer world spirals and spins, expands and contracts around this centre. You are the centre of the universe and everything revolves around you. The holy place, the sacred mountain and the Tree of Life are symbols of the inner state of centredness, stillness and emptiness.[1] These symbols allow you to internalize the significance of the Cross, Mount Fuji, the Bodhi Tree, and help you to live from your inner spiritual centre.

All worldly action takes place around this still centre. But the centre itself is devoid of action, drama, or passion. Your centre is unity, while the outer world is multiplicity. Chuang Tzu said:

When the ten thousand things become one, then we return to the centre, where we have always been.[2]

Your centre is not only a place to withdraw to; it is also the place from where your being takes action. It is not a place where you need anything; it is a place where you have everything you need. When you are in your centre you are not alone, because it is outside of space and time. When you and I are in our centres, we are in the same place because we have transcended the separation of our small selves. When you are perfectly alone, you are completely connected to everyone and everything.

The attachment of the separate self to its own projections precludes our relationship to Life. This attachment creates loneliness, which is born of separation. The separate self is self-obsessed in the narcissistic sense. Separation and loneliness are the outcome of the inability to relate to something other than self.

The deep truth is that you never left your centre and this makes the spiritual journey unique; the spiritual journey is the return to the place that you never left. True centredness takes us beyond loneliness to the realization that we are not separate, and that we have been unified in consciousness all along.

The journey is not from here to there, but from here to here. You are the Axis Mundi – the centre of the world.

Centredness transcends antagonism, dissolves conflict and clarifies projected illusion. The more we are able to connect with our centres, the more we are able to relate to each other in shared truth and purpose. Ultimately we belong to our centre, OM, the Self, where consideration, concern and compassion are inherent qualities. From this still point we are able to receive others, resonate with the feelings of others, empathize with their situations and share our own experiences, emotions and 'being' without prejudice or denial. Maintaining your own centredness allows others to do the same. This has a great impact on many levels – personal, interpersonal, familial, communal, cultural and global. Arnie Mindell, who works to resolve conflicts in some of the major trouble spots of the world, remarks:

The Western white world is terrified of emotions . . . sometimes emotions are very scary. On the other hand without bringing emotions in you'll never be able to negotiate peace treaties. You can see what has happened in Israel and the Middle East, or in Ireland. It is ridiculous to try to make a peace between groups who have a history of hating each other – it never works. We have to have arenas for open forum debate between people who don't like each other to be heard and appreciated, not just logical debate.[3]

There is a growth game that shows you how easy it can be to lose your centre. You need a cushion, a group of people and some space. The cushion represents the thing each person wants most in the world. A member of the group takes the cushion and the rest try to get it. You might start by just pretending but, after a very short while, your centre is in the cushion and you are chasing after it in earnest.

From commerce to religion the same trick has been used time and time again: convince people that they cannot do without X. We allow ourselves to be manipulated, so that our natural tendency towards centring in ourselves is diverted into some futile material gain which leaves us feeling hungry, empty, and lacking.

Your centre contains everything and nothing because it contains all potentialities. Our unique worth as human beings is that we are the link between good and evil, spirit and soul, earth and heaven. To be totally human is to realize our potential to bring together the human and the Divine. Goethe wrote:

> For what the centre brings
> Must obviously be
> That which remains to the end
> And was there from eternity.[4]

What 'was there from eternity' transcends space and time and is eternal. Sri Krishna Prem comments on the *Bhagavad Gita*:

> The Voice of Krishna can be heard only in silence, and as long as the heart is filled with the clamour of desire the silver tones of the Voice cannot be heard. It is only when the outer world becomes utterly dark that the Ray of the Divine Star can be seen by us, for, although It shines eternally, yet it is only when the glaring sunlight of so-called life is eclipsed that we can at first perceive It.

Later, that Star will shine with such a Light that 'if the splendour of a thousand suns were to blaze out together in the sky, that might resemble the glory of that Mahatma,' and not all earth's tumult will be able to deafen us to the majestic rhythm of that Voice, that Voice that reverberates throughout the Eternities as the tides of Being thunder upon the beaches of the worlds.[5]

When you are the centre of the world you have that Voice – the Voice of Krishna, of God, of the Self. Not only hearing that Voice but *becoming* it – that is the arrival at your true centre where the Divine ray shines out of utter darkness.

·THE DARK NIGHT OF THE SOUL·

The dark night of the soul is a way of initiation, a process through which we surrender, deepen and cleanse the soul. It is a ceremony through which we die to all our illusions and enter into Life. Only when the sun is eclipsed can the unaided eye see the sun's corona. The dark night of the soul is the meeting with the Divine that calls for the relinquishing of the small, separate self. Cheapened as the phrase has become in popular speech, the dark night of the soul is often used to describe any deep life trauma or depression; but the dark night is an earthquake in your consciousness where everything is turned on its head and all seems to be eclipsed. Sri Krishna Prem again:

> ... before the bright Path of the Sun can be trodden, the aspirant must enter the valley of gloom, must close his eyes and ears to the light and laughter of life, and must realize in sorrow that all that he is and all that he has is nothing, before he can see and know in joy that within his heart is the All. [6]

The human soul merges into God's Wisdom and Love. It is the complete surrender of the trappings of the self and the following of a single desire, the desire for which all lesser desires have been striving: to become one with the Divine. This requires dropping every attachment, however slight...

> Whether it be a strong wire rope or a slender and delicate thread that holds the bird, it matters not, if it really holds it fast; for, until the cord be broken, the

bird cannot fly. So the soul, held by the bonds of human affections, however slight they may be, cannot, while they last, make its way to God.[7]

... and renouncing all preferences, aversions and self-will in total surrender to the Divine will, since it is only by dropping these attachments that we can embrace unified Consciousness, which is our true and highest nature. We drop the particular for the All and exchange fullness for emptiness.

The goods of God, which are beyond all measure, can only be contained in an empty and solitary heart.[8]

The rigours of the dark night of the soul might seem extreme to the contemporary mind. But when people speak deeply about their lives, they can frequently recount some kind of transcendent experience. Often they will speak of it in a down-to-earth way, without using spiritual language. The key to uncovering a person's deepest, and possibly spiritual, experience is to see where their heart's direction lies. What is the nature of the things that affect them most deeply? Are these things spiritual, emotional, intellectual or material? What do they desire more than anything else? What do they honour in their lives?

Reading the archaic literature on the spiritual journey — the works of the Christian mystics in particular — can make you feel quite irredeemable, as if the fruits of spiritual transformation were beyond your grasp. But try to remember that these were quite ordinary people describing experiences that are available to us all. Although the way appears different today and our accounts may sound different, the essence and the ordeal of the dark night of the soul is essentially the same. The nature of the Divine is eternal.

Your spiritual practice, your love of God, and the means to your full potential are perpetually present in the circumstances of your life. Your life is the path. The key is your heart's direction; the key is love. Sometimes the way is so obvious that we do not see it.

A troubled woman came to Ramakrishna, saying, 'O Master, I do not find that I love God.' And he asked, 'Is there nothing, then, that you love?' To this she answered, 'My little nephew'. And he said to her, 'There is your love and service to God, in your love and service to that child'.[9]

Divine wisdom eclipses the light of the separate soul. An encounter with the Divine inevitably throws your life into turmoil, as you struggle to assimilate the new paradigms of Truth. The darkness that the soul experiences is only dark compared to the reflected light of the Divine. This dark night has the power to transform you absolutely. When you are ready, you do not merely rock the boat of your illusions; you capsize it. When your longing has reached such an intensity of surrender, you understand that your purpose is to manifest Love. The outer world starts to lose its appeal as you turn your energy inwards.

At the beginning, you can feel depressed and withdrawn. You may have nightmares, anxiety and apprehension. It is essential to have support from a spiritually orientated therapist, or guide – a confidant who has made a heartfelt commitment to his or her own spiritual journey. Also you need a supportive environment that is peaceful and contemplative, meditative and compassionate, and a supportive group of kindred spirits.

The dark night of the soul is that place the poet T.S.Eliot evokes:

> I said to my soul, be still, and let the dark come upon you
> Which shall be the darkness of God. As, in a theatre,
> The lights are extinguished, for the scene to be changed
> With a hollow rumble of wings, with a movement of darkness on darkness...
> ... Not lost, but requiring, pointing to the agony
> Of death and birth.
> ... still and still moving
> Into another intensity
> For a further union, a deeper communion
> Through the dark cold and the empty desolation...
> ... In my end is my beginning.[10]

In the same poem Eliot echoes these words of St. John of the Cross:

> If you want to have pleasure in everything,
> You must desire to have pleasure in nothing.
> If you want to possess everything,
> You must desire to possess nothing.

If you want to become all,
You must desire to be nothing.
If you want to know all,
You must desire to know nothing.
If you want to arrive at that which you know not,
You must go by a way which you know not.
If you want to arrive at that which you possess not,
You must go by a way which you possess not.
If you want to arrive at that which you are not,
You must pass through that which you are not. [11]

Your journey through the dark night of the soul is unique. It is a threshold that you are compelled to cross. You have to face all that is dark inside you, all the disowned parts of your psyche that you have previously projected outside and that now turn out to be inside you. The union of the soul with the Divine reveals that the universe is within. This revelation is – in the words of St. Teresa of Avila – like 'water falling from heaven into a river or fountain, when all becomes water, and it is not possible to divide or separate the water of the river from that which fell from heaven; or when a little stream enters the sea so that henceforth there shall be no means of separation'.

· YOUR LIFE IS THE PATH ·

That you must lead your own life is a truth that so often evades us – it is perhaps too obvious. You do not need to search for a path when the life you are leading is already the path. You can attain the Divine only by following your individual destiny. Your life is the path.

This is an age-old insight related in the mythology of the Grail, which has remained the model for the inner landscape of the Western mind for almost two thousand years. In the Arthurian legends, when the knights ride out to their adventures, each discovers his unique oath; which is created as it is experienced:

They thought it would be a disgrace to go forth in a group. Each entered the forest that he had chosen where there was no path and where it was darkest. [12]

There is 'no path' because there has been no 'you' before. The path is only ever found once. The beginning of the *Bhagavad Gita* illustrates this in a passage describing the dejection of the great warrior Arjuna. Krishna counsels Arjuna in a chariot on the field of life. Together in the chariot are God and man – both the human and the Divine, the unification of our two aspects, our duality. Arjuna is dejected because he does not want to meet his destiny. He is acutely aware of the chain of consequences which are intrinsic to life and it has become too painful for him. Nevertheless, Krishna tells Arjuna to surrender to his destiny and live the life that only he can live.

Many guides would have us travel single file, like mules in a pack train, and never leave the trail. He taught us to move forward like the breeze, tasting the berries, greeting the blue jays, learning and loving the whole terrain.

Gary Snyder on Alan Watts

When we look with envy at somebody else's life and wish it were our own, or when we abandon our life for any reason, what part of us is it that considers ourselves so unimportant? Who within us is it that says the universe does not require this life to be led? What right do we have to disregard ourselves like this?

Your life is as important as a field of grass; it is as important as the wind blowing, or as a bird flying; it is important and unique! Instead of seeing your life from the point of view of your pleasure or self-importance, turn it around and ask, 'How can the universe be fulfilled through this life? How do I manifest the Divine?' This is a wholly different perspective on life. What you like or do not like, or what makes you happy or unhappy, becomes much less important. All of these are dichotomies, born of dualities. You become more concerned about your ability to open yourself and say, 'I have no choice. I'm the only me there is to live my life. No one else can do this'. Your life is vital because you *are* life.

When you surrender your life to the Higher Self in service to the Divine, you become an instrument of life; you vivify things. By embracing and living your own life you support and nurture the divine existence. All things are eternal, nothing is born and nothing dies, and you must get on with the unfolding of your life. The small self is not separate from the Higher Self, since everything is divine. The small self flowers into realization in the Higher Self, so you should strengthen your resolve and make the singular decision to lead your own life. As you open to that, life, and death, may be seen from a higher perspective:

> As a man abandons worn-out clothes and acquires new ones, so when the body is worn out a new one is acquired by the Self, who lives within.[13]

•THE DUAL CONDITIONS OF GOOD AND EVIL•

When the opposites arise the Buddha mind is lost.[14]

Morality has so impinged on our consciousness as an accompaniment to spirituality through organized religion, that we may have difficulty seeing that the concepts of good and evil exist only in the world of the opposites. Good and evil are concepts of human understanding and are not of the Divine mind. Darkness is not a thing in itself; it is simply the absence of light. Similarly, evil is not a thing in itself; it is simply the absence of good. In his posthumously published Gnostic work, *The Seven Sermons to the Dead*, Jung wrote:

> Everything that ye entreat from the god-sun begetteth a deed of the devil... Good and evil are united... Each star is a god, and each space that a star filleth is a devil.[15]

The spiritual journey is not a way of conflict; it is the way through conflict. It is participatory and inclusive, not adversarial and exclusive. The path that we must follow is the narrow path between the pairs of opposites. We do not need to do battle with the powers of darkness. Instead we should illuminate, with heart-felt kindness, those dark areas of ourselves.

When enough of us disown our own darkness and point and say, 'You are the evil one,' we create a scapegoat to carry our collective burden. Newspapers contain outpourings of venom towards the 'animals' and 'beasts' that result from our collective disavowal of our dark sides. Evildoers range from adulterers to serial killers, from murderous dictators to rapists. Yet even these people are human beings, capable of realizing the Divine within themselves, capable of opening their hearts to others, and even they have the potential and the capacity for love. When we are courageous enough to descend into our own darkness and face the 'evil' within ourselves, then we release others from having to do it for us.

> Once I had a tremendous experience of evil in my personal therapy. What helped me through it was remembering that feeling states are essentially impersonal: they will pass through you, so long as you do not become attached to them. I had begun to feel like the personification of evil itself. There was no particular issue that I had brought to my session, no particular focus for anger, hatred or anything like that. It took me completely by surprise. I felt my potential for the most base, corrupt, hateful and unfeeling acts imaginable. I understood that I was capable of murder, rape and unspeakable cruelty. All the inhumane acts possible were within me, as unchosen potentialities. It was like draining some ancient lake and finding the most surprising things had been thrown in. I stood with my back to the wall, feeling like the Devil himself.
>
> I pulled myself out for a few seconds and said to my therapist, 'Are you alright with this?'
>
> 'Yes', she said. It was all I needed. I allowed the energy of evil to flow through and out of me, as I would have done any other energy or emotion. I stayed with it until it cleared and left me.

The evil inside ourselves is hard to confront, acknowledge or even admit to and not be frightened of. We should remember that this is where our souls are most in need of healing. We must open our hearts to ourselves first and then, since all healing is self-healing, we help to heal others by our example. 'Everything flowers, from within, of self-blessing,' wrote Galway Kinnell:

> ...sometimes it is necessary
> to reteach a thing its loveliness,
> to put a hand on its brow...
> until it flowers again from within, of self-blessing...[16]

This story illustrates the split in our psyche.

> A Native American grandfather told his grandson that he had two wolves inside him. One was peaceful, loving and nurturing and would not attack

unless it was in real danger. The second wolf was vengeful, full of rage and would attack at the slightest provocation. The grandson asked, 'Which one gets the better of you?' and his granddad replied, 'The one that gets the better of me is the one I feed'.

As soon as we fall out of unity and enter duality, we have good and bad, dark and light, love and fear. We feed whichever wolf we choose to feed, but what do we do with the other one? Should we just ignore it? The answer is that we have to acknowledge it because it is a part of us. It is simply not enough to feed the one we choose. If we do not own the other wolf, we disown a part of ourselves and create an 'orphan' in our consciousness. Rather than rejecting the 'evil' wolf, we can be together with it. This is the wisest way to handle anything that is pushing us off balance: be in the middle of it and let it reveal itself. Usually it turns out to be something other than it appears. When we embrace life we invite transformation; when we shed light we dissolve shadows – this is the way to wholeness. Ramakrishna said:

> I have come to the stage of realization in which I see that God is walking in every human form and manifesting himself alike in the sage and in the sinner.[17]

Although it was necessary in the past to project authority outwards and lead life in response to a set of ethical rules, today we are faced with the deeper responsibility of centring ourselves within. We discover our true authenticity and authority when we look into our open hearts. The light must shine in and through us – then the way is always clear. We discover the compassion to accept another human being, whatever their appearance, and see their divinity. We are all connected; we are all parts of the Whole. When we disavow someone else we deny our totality, our truth, the Self.

> Buddha died and ascended to heaven where he met Saint Peter at the gates of Paradise. Saint Peter naturally invited him in since Buddha had led a very good life. Buddha, however, declined to enter and remarked, 'How can the hand enter and not the rest of the body?' And it is said that he remains there to this day waiting until every last one of us is ready to enter heaven with him.

·THE ROOTS OF DESIRE·

In the ancient *Vedas* – literally 'sacred teaching' – the world of appearances is made up of three *gunas*, or qualities – goodness, passion and ignorance. These three qualities both conceal and are born of Brahman – Absolute non-duality. Goodness represents the inner purity that we need to realize the Self; passion stimulates activity and is regarded as the obstacle to goodness, and ignorance produces immobility, which is needed to overcome passion. According to the *Vedas*, we need to balance these three qualities so that nothing appears in the realm of *maya*, then all is in perfect poise and the Higher Self can be fully realized.

The realization of the Self is such a tremendous undertaking it is little wonder that we can so easily be misled as we journey along the spiritual path. The Chinese Ch'an master Shi Fu observed:

> There are many examples of mistaken lives… Some people go into the mountains and practice, maybe for years. They come to feel that they have gone beyond all greed and hatred. The mind is calm so how could such negatives arise? They may even feel they have attained liberation. So they come down from the mountains and start interacting again in the world. Quite quickly they may get irritated by others, or form some emotional attachments, which they find they cannot handle. Greed and hatred appear and they are forced to recognize that they still have major vexations.[18]

To overcome the second guna of passion we have to consider the roots of desire. What is it that causes us to believe that something outside us will fulfil us in our inner life? What assumptions about incompleteness or inner lack support our attraction towards external things for gratification? What would satisfy us? How could we ever be satisfied?

As ever in the world of duality there are two ways to work with this. We can work with the renunciation of desire, or the fulfilment of desire. Either way will only be of benefit if we deepen further into our awareness of the roots of desire. Where does it come from? What is its true nature? We can find the answer to these questions by remaining still in the midst of the restlessness of desire, by removing the obstacle to our essential goodness. The earth-like quality of ignorance is used to overcome fiery passion – activity and desire – which is the obstacle to purity.

Desire, of course, is endless and, curiously, the satisfaction of desire never satiates us. The interminable nature of desire is revealed in the fact that it is never diminished. In fact, desire feeds off itself – desire increases desire. Should desire ever truly be fulfilled, desire would end.

• NO-SEEKING •

With notable exceptions – Ramakrishna, Ramana Maharshi, Alan Watts and in more recent times, Da Free John (now Avatar Adi Da Samraj) – the point is seldom made that in the ultimate desire – the desire for the realization of the Self, which would extinguish all desires – we are as caught as ever in the quality of passion. How are we to attain the state of no-seeking? How are we to drop the final desire?

Since to realize the Self we must transcend the seeker, the answer is to start in the place where you are not seeking. To start from where you are not seeking creates a Zen *koan* – an impossible question that provokes intuitive insight. Who is the seeker who is not seeking? What is the colour black when it is not black? What is the sound of one hand clapping? These questions demand a spontaneous answer from your being; an intellectual response will never do.

When we drop progress, frustration, competitiveness, aggression, striving and desire – seeking in all its diverse forms – what is left? In a Zen story:

> An elderly holy man, eager to gain enlightenment, came to see Buddha. He carried two gifts, one in each hand. As he approached, Buddha cried out, 'Drop it!' and the holy man let go of one of the gifts. As he came further, Buddha again cried out, 'Drop it!' and he let go of the other one. 'Drop it!' cried Buddha again and the empty-handed holy man stood perplexed, then he smiled.

Always be aware of the limitations of your spiritual practice. Whenever a spiritual method assumes the existence of limitations, you are limited by the method. The true spiritual path is beyond all limitations. The Self is already here. There is nothing to seek.

· RITUAL AND BEING AT OM ·

OM is the sound and expression of our awakening, the One Consciousness, the Truth and our soul's identity in God. As such it stands as a symbol, both in sound and form, of our spiritual home.

The outward practices of meditation, retreat, *mantra*, yoga, contemplation, or any other spiritual practice, only serve the being at OM. We need quiet time to centre ourselves, to attune and to focus our awareness. Love yourself enough to give yourself this time. After a while, you will be able to maintain your centre and focus in the world, without getting caught up in the whirlwind of interaction.

It is necessary to establish a practice and stick with it – and let it go when you are called to. Always remember that you are more important than any of your achievements and that it is a characteristic of the spiritual to challenge your attachment to your accomplishments. When the small self starts to glorify itself in the light of spiritual success, you should be cautious!

Ritual is one of our fundamental needs because it is a way of bridging the inner and outer worlds. So many of our acts are symbolic, from shaking hands to kneeling in prayer. Turning our actions consciously towards the Divine is the purpose of spiritual ritual. Any act can become a ritual when we do it consciously. When specific ritual acts are called for, they may emerge from our deep unconscious. Communing with a departed loved one at a waterfall, creating an altar at home, cleaning a room with reverence or driving a car with consideration are all effective rituals. As we deepen in spiritual practices, it is most important that we honour our deepest impulses to perform ritual. The call to ritual is an invitation to participate in and celebrate the gifts of Life. Ritual is an opportunity to transcend the small self and commune with the Divine within.

What now seems to you opaque, you will make transparent with your blazing heart.

Rainer Maria Rilke

All things are sacred. In ritual we recognize this sacredness and develop a reverence for life. Where ritual leads, simply follow and say yes – OM. The most ordinary acts can be consciously enacted as ritual. We can raise the routine and the ordinary to new levels of reverence and honour, imbuing our lives with sacred significance. Through ritual we externalize the deep unconscious and touch the Divine in the human world.

·The Lure of Quietism·

During this stage, we may experience a desire to withdraw from the world. The deep awareness of our centre brings with it a sense of self-sufficiency, self-containment, and self-abiding. The attraction to seclusion can be irresistible. The lure of quietism attracts many, but choosing it often brings about a false self-satisfaction. The ego then tries to seduce us with the idea that having worked so hard, we have earned a holiday from the spiritual and from the Truth. Once lured, the seduction deepens: 'Why not stay for good?' But the spiritual path is imbued with natural laws and one of them is that we cannot use its rewards for selfish ends. To try to do so breeds restlessness and disillusionment. On the spiritual journey, we must keep moving and be ever becoming. Thomas Merton wrote:

> The truest solitude is not something outside you, not an absence of men or of sound around you; it is an abyss opening up in the centre of your soul. And this abyss of interior solitude is created by a hunger that will never be sampled with any created things.[19]

So, the experience of oneness with the Self is followed by a returning.

> When you go
> to the dark place
> you must come back
> singing
> the note inscribed
> on your palm
> the song written
> on your hand
> the way trees
> grow about the
> shape of the wind.[20]

· Part 4 ·

THE FLIGHT OF CONSCIOUSNESS

RETURNING TO THE SOURCE

This 'I am' is an announcement: it is not the real. What the real is, I am not telling you, because words negate that. Whatever I am telling you is not the truth, because it has come out of that 'I am'. The fact is, I cannot describe reality to you, I cannot explain it, because it is beyond expression.

Sri Nisargadatta Maharaj

Consciousness is interpenetrating, eternally emerging, like a great ocean of infinite waves. The ten stages of the spiritual journey merge into one another. From the cosmic viewpoint our individual lives are like tiny prisms of light in a kaleidoscope – with just a tiny twist everything shifts and alters.

In the penultimate stage of the sacred journey, we try to elucidate the path of return, deepen in our understanding of spiritual transformation, and penetrate the silence between the words. Words are momentary forms arising in silence and they interact with the solitary silence to resonate in the heart, pulse in the body and shine on the soul. But spiritual truth is more than thought or word, feeling or experience, intellect or intuition, sensation or substance. The deepest teaching comes out of deep stillness, silence and receptivity – all characteristics of our true nature. The only path is the path of our heart.

•FINDING WORDS FOR THE WORDLESS•

In talking about spiritual truth we find words for what is wordless; we speak of that which cannot be spoken.

Once there was a wall. Occasionally someone would come and climb the wall and when they reached the top they would look over, smile and slip over. They were never seen again. Eventually people became curious and they came to the wall to watch. They wondered what was on the other side. They began to recognize the ones that came to climb the wall by the faraway look in their eyes and their disinterest in the world. One day a young man, who they recognized by these signs, came to climb the wall. As he set off, they wrapped ropes around his legs. When he reached the top of the wall, he smiled. It was a smile of rapture. Just as he was about to slip over the wall, they pulled on the ropes and brought him down to the ground. Filled with curiosity they questioned him: 'What was it like? What is on the other side?' But none of their questions were ever answered because the young man was struck dumb. He never regained the power of speech.

Not only can words dishonour spiritual truth and pale its true meaning, but it may be impossible to use them to convey any deep sense of the spiritual. The spiritual teacher Krishnamurti observed:

> ...the door is there. But the description of the door is not the door, and when you get emotionally involved in the description you don't see the door. This description might be a word or a scientific treatise or a strong emotional response; none of these is the door itself... The description is never the described.[1]

Words are like traps. They should catch and convey living concepts and then, like traps, be put aside. In Chuang Tzu's words:

> The purpose of words is to convey ideas. When the ideas are grasped, the words are forgotten. Where can I find a man who has forgotten words?[2]

The written word may be an even greater obstacle to wisdom than the spoken word. Over two thousand years ago, the Greek philosopher Plato wrote:

> ... this invention [letters] will produce forgetfulness in the minds of those who learn to use it, because they will not practice their memory. Their trust in writing, produced by external characters, which are no part of themselves, will discourage the use of their own memory within them. You have invented an elixir not of memory, but of reminding; and you offer your pupils the appearance of wisdom, not true wisdom, for they will read many things without instruction and will therefore seem to know many things, when they are for the most part ignorant and hard to get along with, since they are not wise, but only appear wise.[3]

To forget words and make life our own through spontaneity, is to connect fully with life. This is a total relationship to life with nothing held back; a life without words, concepts, models and beliefs, a life of integration without the veil of interpretation.

While ultimate reality cannot be spoken *of*, it can be spoken *by*. Our spirit utters our words when we open fully to the Divine and surrender to the Source of Life. We are inspired, filled with spirit, and the key is that we do not know what we are saying, before we say it. We become spontaneous, uninhibited, and unashamed. Then we are the listener, as well as the speaker. Before our words can have any spiritual substance, we must *become* what we cannot speak of. The *Kena Upanishad*:

> What cannot be spoken with words, but that whereby words are spoken. Know that alone to be Brahman, the Spirit and not what people here adore.[4]

At the Source, we discover that the voice of Brahman, of God, can speak through us. We can offer ourselves back to the Source which offers the gift of life and allow the words to flow from our hearts to our mouths.

We have to work very subtly with spiritual truths to arrive at a far deeper understanding than our egoic self will allow. If we only listen to words through the filter of our contracted self, they can never instil in us their true meaning. As we attempt to realize Truth, we should reach down deeply into our being and connect with a living sense of what spiritual concepts represent and what they are trying to express. The question we should always keep in our awareness is, 'How should this be lived?' Any attempt by the ego to reduce these ideas – even to understand them – should be rejected. Spiritual ideas should inhabit the borderline of our consciousness, because they stimulate the expansion of our being.

·HOW IS LIFE FULFILLED?·

When we have developed through the spiritual stages and deepened inside ourselves, a new quality of being begins to emerge. We begin to sense the Source of Life, which is at our core. We are more than the experience of the senses or the meaning of words, neither body or mind. We are the creation of consciousness returning to the Source of Life. How are we to live this insight? The challenge is beyond words or experience. We seek the very nature of existence and we ask, 'How is life fulfilled?' It is never sufficient simply to have insight, that intuitive leap of consciousness, the spiritual aha! Our flight of consciousness needs to be grounded in our commitment to the spiritual journey.

To sustain the insight, 'I am Life' we must abandon subtle forms of holding. We must release attachments, sever the psychic cord that triggers the birth of transformation, see things as they are – which is beyond all being and non-being – and practise forgiveness without reserve.

These four aspects of the spiritual path, which we must consider in this stage, appear to describe the life of a genuine saint. But when we look around us we can see these qualities reflected in ordinary life – in the check-out assistant at the supermarket, in the person who stops to help, in the person who holds our child's hand to get them safely off the train, in the person who does not bear resentment, and in numerous acts of kindness which we can witness each day. Enlightenment is ordinary life and if you hold your centre and deepen into the Self – if it has not happened to you already – one day you will be handing over a cheque at the bank and you will look into the bank clerk's eyes and see God behind the security glass.

· NOWHERE TO STAND ·

When we stand somewhere, we are identified with a personal view to which we are attached. We are convinced that how we see it is how it is. But that is not true. How you see it is how it appears to you and how I see it is how it appears to me. We are each of us describing a part of the whole.

Our fixed mind creates our sharp edges, which are the entrenched, unforgiving, unyielding aspects of the self. This is the edge that we need to work at. Arguments, disagreements and conflicts illumine this area for us. In relationships of all kinds, we can do some of our best work on our fixedness to where we stand.

When we stand somewhere, our awareness is closed and our understanding is incomplete. But, when we stand nowhere, we stand everywhere. We are no longer fixed; we are able to see the other side because we are unattached to a point of view. The insecurity of life is that there truly is nowhere to stand. But our conditioning requires us to be something, be somebody, stand somewhere, have an opinion, hold a position, to define and be defined. Nevertheless, our position is not who we truly are – it is only how we defend ourselves – and it brings us misery, limitation and loss. Our dilemma is how to live lightly with the roles, with our character, with our activity in the world and yet stand nowhere.

When you stand nowhere, you are everywhere. We break down the barriers of separation between self and other. The attachments, which cause us misery, are gone; we no longer have reasons for offence or anger, or the means to create pain in our lives. We can be with someone without clinging to our separateness and defending our corner. So much of life is spent fighting, justifying, defending and struggling. We want to dominate, to be better than the other, liked by the other, envied by the other. When we stand somewhere, we are blinkered from truth.

· WHERE DO YOU GET CAUGHT? ·

Life is our great teacher. Our teacher may be inner or outer, playful or profound, apparent or hidden. Whenever we get caught in the snares of selfhood and its attendant states of self-importance and self-delusion, our teacher is there to release us. Learn to recognize life's lessons – a book, a smile, a sunset, a friend, an enemy, a saucepan, a rock, an ant – anything can teach us at any time; so be watchful!

A lesson may come through driving along in a car when suddenly a truck pulls out in front of us, or buying something in a shop where the assistant is rude to us, or waiting for someone who does not arrive punctually, or socializing when someone says a hurtful word to us. Teaching comes in a multitude of guises. It is important for us to know where we get caught. It is important for us to recognize our lesson and to know how we meet it.

How we meet life depends on our separateness and how we perceive the world. Chuang Tzu says:

If a man is crossing a river
And an empty boat collides with his own skiff,

Even though he be a bad-tempered man
He will not become very angry.
But if he sees a man in the boat,
He will shout at him to steer clear.
If the shout is not heard, he will shout again,
And yet again, and begin cursing.
And all because there is somebody in the boat.
Yet if the boat were empty,
He would not be shouting, and not angry.
If you empty your own boat
Crossing the river of the world,
No one will oppose you,
No one will seek to harm you.[5]

Life works at our edge, where we are least expecting and where we are fixed in our self-importance. Often the work of the teacher is invisible to the outside and only known to the inner self, as in this story about Zen Master Kasan. Then it is a matter of deep personal integrity for us to follow the teaching.

Kasan was asked to officiate at the funeral of a provincial lord. He had never met lords and nobles before so he was nervous. When the ceremony started, Kasan sweated. Afterwards, when he had returned, he gathered his pupils together. Kasan confessed that he was not yet qualified to be a teacher for he lacked the sameness of bearing in the world of fame that he possessed in the secluded temple. Then Kasan resigned and became the pupil of another master. Eight years later he returned to his former pupils, enlightened.[6]

• RE-EMERGENCE AFTER THE SECOND DEATH •

At birth, we experience the first death, which is the ending of all that has preceded our emergence into this life. The first death brings us into the physical body and begins the creation of the small separate self, the process of character defences, and our models of experience.

The second death is the birth of the Self, the Higher Self, and it awaits everyone. The second death is the release of our attachment to the self and the realization of our spiritual potential. This requires the severing of the psychic cord that attaches us to the past.

If we want to die to our old self and invite transformation, we must consciously choose to do so. Implied in that choice is a deep acceptance of what that transformation brings. Our total willingness, combined with grace, produces this transformation.

The Tibetan bardo system offers a wonderful insight into the nature of existence. A bardo is a threshold, an opening – literally an 'in-between state'.

When man is for a moment silent and ready to listen, the God who speaks through the voice of the Self tells him to die... The death God counsels is the death of unconscious life and a rebirth into a life of conscious choice... This voice can be silenced. Then death becomes the living death of those who have all they want to have and know all they want to know, and so have died to the life of transformation.

Frances G. Wickes

The system teaches that all existence passes eternally through a process of change. A lifetime is made up of three bardos. First, arising, when individual life appears and then develops between conception and birth. Second, roaming, when we create an identity for ourselves and the course of our life unfolds. Third, dissolution, when the body and the mind deteriorate through old age until the point when we leave physical form.

What is surprising in this system is that the conditions after death parallel those in life. We are said to go through arising, roaming and dissolution after death, before we emerge into life again. Thus life and the afterlife resemble each other. This expansive perspective, transcending birth and death, helps us see how strong our attachment is to our 'roaming'. We think we are solely our personal identity and our individual life, when we are so much more.

The impulse that urges our unconscious to emerge into consciousness and strives to bring about the new birth eventually results in the death of the self. When we surrender to the unconscious, we undertake the descent into all that is dark within us, which is our shadow. The shadow is the unseen, the repellent, the terrifying, and the unknown. This descent is the journey into the dark abyss to reunite with the unconscious. It is the experience of entering the darkness of the underworld and re-emerging into the light in wholeness and renewal.

The abyss is the life-giving womb, from which we are born out of transformation. It is the place to which inner work directs us for it is the meeting with our True Self which makes us complete. The Jungian analyst Robert A. Johnson comments:

> No one can be anything but a partial being, ravaged by doubt and loneliness, unless he has close contact with his shadow... Assimilating one's shadow is the art of catching up on those facets of life that have not been lived out adequately. Wholeness implies that we must find those parts of our self that are missing in life.[7]

•SEEING THINGS AS THEY ARE•

We tend to see the world as we are. Since we love certain aspects of ourselves and hate others, our relationship to the self is ambivalent and selective. When we stop selecting – dividing the lovable from the unlovable – we are faced with the whole of ourselves to love. When we love ourselves totally, we see the world through the eyes of love: we see things as they are.

We have to free ourselves from our illusory perception of the world. To see things as they really are, we have to transcend the opposites and resist our chronic tendency to criticize and judge. This tendency stems from our dualistic model of the world. At the very root of our judgement lies the question of good and evil. Joseph Campbell tells this story:

> Once in India I thought I would like to meet a major guru or teacher face to face. So I went to see a celebrated teacher named Sri Krishna Menon, and the first thing he said to me was, 'Do you have a question?'
>
> The teacher in this tradition always answers questions. He doesn't tell you anything you are not yet ready to hear. So I said, 'Yes, I have a question. Since in Hindu thinking everything in the universe is a manifestation of divinity itself, how should we say no to anything in the world? How should we say no to brutality, to stupidity, to vulgarity, to thoughtlessness?' And he answered, 'For you and for me – the way is to say yes.' We then had a wonderful talk on this theme of the affirmation of all things.[8]

How can we reconcile saying 'yes', with our perceptions of misery, evil, and cruelty in the world? Saying 'yes' to all things is seeing things as they are. We cannot split God up into what is holy and unholy, divine and not divine, since God is everything. When we judge things as good or evil, we deny parts of the whole. Rumi said:

Out beyond ideas of wrongdoing and rightdoing,
there is a field. Will you meet me there?
When the soul lies down in that grass,
the world is too full to talk about.
Ideas, language, even the phrase *each other* (italics mine)
Doesn't make any sense.9

It is impossible to sort the events of our lives into 'good' and 'bad' experiences. Our awareness of the process of life reveals the 'good' transforming into 'bad' and the 'bad' into 'good.' No judgement on life sustains deep scrutiny.

A man with a good job lived in a large house with his family. When his firm went bankrupt, he lost his job and had to sell his house. After a while he thought, 'Now I can do what I always wanted to do'. So he bought some land with the money from the house, started to farm it and experienced great fulfilment. His son suffered bad injuries while ploughing one of the fields on his tractor. The skill of the doctors at the nearby hospital saved his son's life. However, his leg was so badly injured that it had to be amputated. His son made a brilliant recovery, but he was unable to play his much-loved sport or work on the farm. However, through the amputation the boy experienced a personal transformation. He visited the hospital and talked to the young people who had had similar operations to his own. He developed great sensitivity and rapport and announced to his father that he had discovered his life's work...

We must see the light in the dark and the dark in the light. This is illustrated in the yin yang symbol. The two interlocking fishes of the symbol – one light, the other dark – each contain a spot of the other's colour. The whole is represented as a combination of these two energies and each is in the process of transformation into the other. In the mystic heart of all the major world religions we find various forms of the same idea, encouraging us to see the good in evil and the evil in good, and the compassion that transcends both.

I once went to a Tantric meditation retreat deep in the countryside. I was feeling acutely sensitive to the brutality of nature and the poignancy of creation and destruction. To me the world seemed to consist of good and evil and the two were clearly separate.

We were given a meditation exercise. We had to find a place and simply *be there* – opening up and receiving the totality of it all. I found a beautiful little hollow and lay down under the shining sun. I let in the sunshine, the smell of the pungent grass, the soothing purr of the gentle breeze and practised expanding my consciousness.

After a while, my thoughts turned to my problem. I watched the birds, the squirrels, a fox – the countryside was teeming with wildlife. Incredulously, I looked up to see the vision of a huge Buddha filling the sky. The Buddha encompassed everything and within him everything was connected. A feeling of great calm came over me. I understood that everything was just right.

When we can see things as they are, we have let go of our judgements and our models. As we free the world from our prejudices, we ourselves are liberated. Life is beyond separation. We can notice how we need the world to conform to our models, witness the tourniquet of our belief systems and the stranglehold of our models. We can see this in others too and then reflect it back on ourselves. Even seeing one beautiful thing, a glimpse of light, or a single act of unselfconscious generosity in another is enough to remind us that we all are divine.

I led a workshop in Europe, which was attended by people from many different countries. In the last session, I asked each of the participants to share something from their Higher Selves. There was a long silence and then one-by-one, each shared a transcendental experience, a spiritual insight, or a deep understanding. Throughout this process one woman remained silent. After a lengthy silence I spoke her name. She started as if she had received a jolt and explained that she had never had a spiritual experience and she suspected that the spiritual journey was not meant for her. Earlier that morning, I had asked her to do me a favour and she had agreed. That day was the end of the workshop, so it was practically certain that I would never see her again. She would return to her country and I to mine. So there was nothing for her to gain from doing a favour for me. I pointed this out and suggested she start looking for her Higher Self in that one selfless act. For a minute she was quiet. Then she looked up, her face beaming shyly. She looked like she had been given a gift.

God is never far from us, but always deep within us. We can always find our deepest Self in the very best in us.

·THE MIRACLE OF FORGIVENESS·

Total forgiveness comes out of the profound surrender of self and a deep merging with the Higher Self. To forgive is to let go of the hard crust of resentment and victim-mentality, which protects and sustains the small self. We must not get caught in the bitterness of our suffering, which perpetuates the double role of victim-perpetrator.

A single act of forgiveness causes a transformation of consciousness. When we falsely forgive, either to make ourselves feel better or to manipulate the other, resentment still flourishes and waits for the next offence. If we practise letting go of hurt, expanding beyond our habitual reactions and seeing ourselves in the other, then we may transcend the cycle of offence, resentment, and forgiveness.

A waterfall, as it cascades down, gives birth to thousands of droplets each second. Although eventually dissolving into the body of the river, which flows into the ocean, each individual droplet is wonderfully unique for a brief time. We are the droplet; we are also the river and the ocean. We are both the forgiver and the forgiven. The Sufi master Hazrat Inayat Khan wrote:

> I have known good and evil, sin and virtue, right and wrong; I have judged and been judged; I have passed through birth and death, joy and sorrow, heaven and hell; and in the end I realized that I am in everything and everything is in me.[10]

Knowing 'I am in everything and everything is in me' is the ultimate responsibility and the ultimate truth, which brushes aside the last veil: the created no longer, but the creator. This supremely transcendent insight is the spiritual condition for nirvana, for heaven itself. As the Jesus of the *Gnostic Gospels* says:

> When you make the two as one... then you will enter the kingdom.[11]

· THREE DIFFERENT PATHS ·

There is a saying: 'Ecstasy is the meal, service is the offering.' When we reach the stage of returning to the Source, we discover our bliss. We sit in being-ness and experience the ecstasy of existence. The response is devotion and it arises out of gratitude, compassion and love – the flowering of our humanness.

We feel compelled to make an offering and so we offer ourselves in service to the Divine. Since we are no longer separate from existence, we serve it. We find our purpose and fulfilment in our surrender to the Divine will and in service to Life. The suffering and the joy of others become our own. Ramakrishna, who followed many religious paths to fulfilment, said:

> There are three different paths to reach the Highest: the path of I, the path of Thou, and the path of Thou and I. According to the first, all that is, was, or ever shall be is I, my higher Self. In other words, I am, I was, and I shall be forever in Eternity. According to the second, Thou art, O Lord, and all is Thine. And according to the third, Thou art the Lord, and I am Thy servant, or Thy son. In the perfection of any of these three ways, a man will find God.[12]

Each of these ways is a spiritual path but only one transcends the illusion of separateness and that is the first: 'the path of I.' Nothing less than the transcendence of this final illusion – namely the manifestation of opposites – is required for entry into the kingdom. It is the release not only from false identity, but also from identity itself. As the ancient *Vedas* describe it: TAT TVAM ASI – that thou art. In other words what you are is both the 'I' and the transcendence of the 'I' – the realization of the Self that is beyond duality.[13]

My struggle against God had been long and hard. I had always pitted my will against the Divine Will. I had a vision of my death: I was in a forest and it was night. I was walking towards a house, which was brightly lit from within. I looked through the window and entered through the front door. His figure was awe-inspiring – a huge swaggering Samurai in full armour and helmet with a giant sword. I pulled out my own sword, which was tiny in comparison, and we began a fierce fight that lasted some time. I became increasingly exhausted. I realized that this Samurai was playing with me. He could kill me at any time. Smarting from the futility of it all, I renewed my attack on him. With a mighty thrust he delivered a fatal blow to my abdomen and I fell...

...I was pure consciousness, no body, no self... nothing but consciousness ...drifting serenely in space. A long way ahead was an object I couldn't see as yet. As I came closer, I saw that it was a goblet, a chalice, which tilted towards me and poured sparkling, glinting water into my being. In that moment I knew that death was the same as life. I knew that nothing had changed. It felt like the cosmic joke. Death and life were the same and life was everlasting.

FREEDOM

You have had the nerve to be born human, and you are delighted. But this body undergoes myriads of changes that never come to an end, and does it not afford occasion for joys incalculable? Therefore the sage enjoys himself in that from which there is no possibility of separation, and by which all things are preserved. He considers early death or old age, his beginning and his ending, all to be good, and in this other men imitate him. How much more will they do so in regard to that on which all things depend, and from which every transformation arises!

Chuang Tzu

All endings are beginnings. All life is a returning, a meeting, a resolving and a going on. In our returning is our completion, in our completion is our wholeness, in our wholeness is our freedom. In the cycle of spiritual transformation we undergo a re-alignment of our souls, a re-centring of our hearts and a total re-orientation to the Self.

The final stage completes the lessons of the journey of the individual soul on the spiritual path and the merging with the Universal Soul as the fulfilment of the spiritual journey. We discover the extraordinary in the ordinary, find the courage to be unseen, let go of the final clinging of the small self and see the world as it is. Ultimately, even God will disappear and only You will remain.

·FINDING THE EXTRAORDINARY IN THE ORDINARY·

In the last illustration of *Kakuan's Ten Bulls*, the herdsman – who symbolizes the individual soul – returns to the market place – which symbolizes ordinary life. He is surrounded by existence in its manifold forms. Mingling with the people in the hustle and bustle of the market place, he has now risen above all desire. He has become one with his True Nature. His enlightenment causes everyone he looks upon to become enlightened. The Jungian therapist, Frances G. Wickes writes:

You come back to the same old life; but the old is now the new because a new concept reanimates and transforms it... We speak of the once-born and the twice-born, but in reality life is a process of deaths and rebirths. We must die to become... God must be brought to birth in the soul again and again...[1]

Returning to ordinary life, we find the extraordinary in the ordinary. We are in the world, but not of the world. We have died to the old life and we can now see the divine play, God's *lila*, and the world reflecting God. Our actions are light, flowing out of the clarity and the emptiness of non-action. Since we are already fulfilled, we seek no satisfaction from the world. Since we are already free, we seek nothing extraordinary and are content with ordinary life.

·THE COURAGE TO BE UNSEEN·

Spiritual realization is an inner event and sustaining it requires inner strength and discipline. Practising constancy and humility sustain us in our True Nature. We are unseen, unknown, non-seeking and quietly blissful. The Indian saint Shankara wrote:

Even though his mind is dissolved in Brahman, he is fully awake, but free from the ignorance of waking life. He is fully conscious, but free from any craving. Such a man is said to be free even in this life. For him, the sorrows of this world are over. Though he possesses a finite body, he remains united with the infinite. His heart knows no anxiety. Such a man is said to be free even in this life.[2]

Usually you will not be ready to be unseen, until you have experienced 'being seen'.[3] You must have experienced some acknowledgement, made an impact on the world, and felt that your existence has affected others. If we seek to transcend what we have not yet attained, then we will not succeed. Psychological growth provides the foundation for spiritual development. Personal flaws are magnified, not transcended, on the spiritual journey. The child grows into an adult, but it is by no means inevitable that an adult will grow into a spiritual seeker.

Most of us have been raised and conditioned to expect and strive for an eternal 'childhood' of longing and satisfaction. Our lives are measured by the extent to which we can satisfy our material desires. But the cycle of satisfaction following increasingly shortened longing grows monotonous, so we introduce excitement, or more usually, the promise of excitement. This cycle binds us to childish desire. Adulthood becomes an extension of childhood through an intensified hunger for excitement, escalating tantalization, and sophisticated longing. Becoming a spiritual adult requires putting down the things of our childhood, meeting new challenges and making new choices.

As we pass through the stages of spiritual life – from child to adult, from adult to Self-realization – there are particular needs. For the child, the needs are emotional and physical nourishment, containment and safety, intimacy and acknowledgement, and, most of all, love. For the adult, the needs are empowerment and ability, the maturation of emotional and physical needs, expansion and will, and, most of all, living a unique life fully. For the spiritual adult, the needs are courage, wisdom, love, and compassion.

Do you have the courage to be unknown, unseen, and unrecognized? Do you have the strength to break your addiction to the drama of life? Can you embrace the reality of your Higher Self? Spiritual invisibility means not minding that most people will not understand how you are living.

We learn to accept invisibility through the processes of discovery, honesty, and the breaking down of separation. We are then intimately bound in a relationship with Life. Sri Nisargadatta Maharaj said:

> There is no chaos in the world except the chaos that your mind creates. It is self-created in the sense that at its very centre is the false idea of oneself as a thing different and separate from other things. In reality you are not a thing nor separate from other things. You are the infinite potentiality, the inexhaustible possibility. Because you are, all can be. The universe is but a partial manifestation of your limitless capacity to become.[4]

Our small separate self can only dissolve in the light of this realization. All our cravings can now be seen as insubstantial and unreal. It will never be possible to enter into invisibility while we still want to be special. A Course in Miracles states:

Specialness always makes comparisons. It is established by a lack seen in another, and maintained by searching for, and keeping clear in sight, all lacks it can perceive. This does it seek, and this it looks upon. And always whom it thus diminishes would be your saviour, had you not chosen to make of him a tiny measure of your specialness instead. Against the littleness you see in him you stand as tall and stately, clean and honest, pure and unsullied, by comparison with what you see. Nor do you understand it is yourself that you diminish thus.[5]

When we distinguish between special and not special, we lose sight of intrinsic worth. When we distinguish between good and evil, we lose sight of absolute good. Original good is unselfconscious good. If you do something that is good and you think, 'Look how good I am', how good *are* you? What is a purely good act? It is an act with no self-consciousness – goodness must come *through* you. *The Tao Te Ching* states:

A truly good man is not aware of his goodness,
And is therefore good.
A foolish man tries to be good,
And is therefore not good.[6]

'Trying' to be good contains a contradiction. We do not have to try to be what we already are.

We put a lot of work into our façades and most of us have very well constructed ones. Consider how much of your energy goes into supporting your image and making an impression on other people. Consider why you spend so much energy trying to bolster your sense of worth, pleasing others, and maintaining your habit of outward orientation. In this stage you completely reverse your orientation. All of the energy turns inward. You take back all the power that has gone into creating an impression on other people and you are no longer self-conscious or consistent. Invisibility is beyond self-consciousness. Invisibility is spontaneity and authenticity. Da Free John (Avatar Adi Da Samraj) writes:

There is only the ordinary... The man of understanding... has no image. At times he denies. At times he asserts. At times he asserts what he has already denied. At times he denies what he has already asserted… His wisdom is vanished… He is of interest to no one. He is fascinating. He is unnoticed. Since no one understands, how could they notice him?[7]

·LETTING GO OF EVERYTHING·

To let go we need to clear old resentments. Resentment is firmly rooted in our emotional histories and represented in sentiments such as, 'I wasn't loved' and 'I wasn't seen'. We need to commit ourselves to the inner journey of emotional clearing, acceptance and forgiveness to achieve the transcendence that is necessary for spiritual transformation. This process itself is the healing which prepares us for freedom.

You cannot realize your wholeness while clinging to the world of duality, where everything has an opposite. This creates imbalance and you veer off the spiritual path. Clinging shows itself in your greed, your lust, your intellectual views, your material attainment, your need to be special – the list is endless.

No one but you can make a valid assessment of your clinging and attachment. Others can make a qualified guess if they know you well; but it is no more than a guess, because others can never know you intimately enough. Even you may not know yourself intimately enough. You can ask, 'How would my life be if I lost everything?'; but do you truly know the answer and would any unenlightened answer ever be fixed and constant? Consider the questions, 'What conditions would have to be fulfilled for me to die happily?' or 'What would I like to be doing if this was the end of the world?' When you consider your life as a whole, you often think of the most euphoric, transcendent, or intensely pleasurable moments. You may also remember those 'special' moments of great rapture and delight, when the small self was totally forgotten. But what of the rest of life: the routine moments and the mundane moments? What does it say about your inner life that you refer solely to outer events to define your inner experience? DT Suzuki writes:

Perfect freedom is obtained only when our egotistic thoughts are not read into life and the world is accepted as it is, as a mirror reflects a flower as a flower.[8]

Letting go of everything is perfect surrender and requires the courage to be, in Karlfried Graf Durckheim's evocative phrase, 'transparent to transcendence': you reveal yourself by allowing God *through* you. You give everything to consciousness and become invisible while God becomes visible. The price of freedom is the relinquishment of everything to which you are attached. In her commentary on the descent into the underworld of the Goddess Inanna, Sylvia Brinton Perera writes:

> [Unveiling] suggests the removal of old illusions and false identities that may have served in the upper world, but which count for nothing in the Netherworld. There one stands naked before the all-seeing eyes of the dark goddess. The unveiling means being stripped bare, the unveiling of the goddess to herself – the original striptease. It suggests a need to be utterly exposed, undefended, open to having one's soul searched by the eye of death, the dark eye of the Self.[9]

Like the money we keep aside for the unexpected, like the breath we keep in our lungs when we exhale – the small self retains a little piece of itself. But if we hold back even the tiniest bit, we are not truly here. The slightest imbalance and we fall back into the world of duality and illusion.

For me once, that tiny bit was called 'Eric'. I had put in some years on my spiritual journey. My inner world had become a kaleidoscope of parts, conflicting views and indecision. I could be exalted one minute and crushed the next. I was passing swiftly through the realms of the selves – those parts of the small 'me' that required acknowledgment to be at peace. I was going through a radical transition and felt very uncomfortable with my life. Everything was somehow 'wrong'. I was practising slow walking meditation with a group, when I fell down unexpectedly. I felt like a stumbling toddler and the unforgiving 'me' was outraged. I felt embarrassed at first, but then overwhelming feelings of despair and desolation came over me that were out of all proportion to what had happened. Falling down seemed to symbolize everything I was getting wrong in my life.

I fled from the building where the others remained walking slowly. I threw myself on the earth outside and, beating it with my fists, I cried to the sky,

'What do I have to do?'

'Love everyone', came the reply from deep inside.

This plunged me into deeper despair. In anguish I tearfully cried back, 'Even Eric?'

Eric was my adversary-helper at that time. He was the 'teacher' who was pushing all my buttons. A highly conventional controlling type, he was, to my eyes, the stereotypical second-in-command. He relayed orders and controlled the petty cash at the place where I worked. I would spend large sums of money in expenses and, whenever I tried to claim my money back, Eric would profess to have no money or claim that he had something more pressing to do. In a multitude of ways he would fob me off and get me to come back later. I had grown to hate him for the feelings of powerlessness that were in me and for which I held him responsible.

It seems ridiculous now, but Eric was my sticking point. He was the only thing in the world I hated. I had given that much of myself to him. Learning to accept, forgive and love Eric was my 'edge' – the place where I was most challenged to be in my heart. The key to moving through this painful period was for me to see that I was hurting myself in hating him. To forgive him, forgive myself, and move beyond this disabling conflict, I had to face up to the disempowering and unforgiving aspects of myself, acknowledge them, and let them go.

This is where all is finally shed, where everything has to go, without exception. Fulfilment and renunciation are not opposites; we live our lives fully in the outside world while renouncing the world of *samsara* – existence without enlightenment – on the inside. Renunciation frees us to live fully unattached to life and its outcome. Buddha said:

I consider the positions of kings and rulers as that of dust motes. I observe treasures of gold and gems as so many bricks and pebbles. I look upon the finest silken robes as tattered rags. I see myriad worlds of the universe as small seeds of fruit, and the greatest lake in India as a drop of oil on my foot. I perceive the teachings of the world to be the illusions of magicians. I discern the highest conception of emancipation as a golden brocade in a dream, and view the holy path of the illuminated ones as flowers appearing in one's eyes. I see meditation as a pillar of a mountain, Nirvana as a nightmare of daytime. I look upon the judgement of right and wrong as the serpentine dance of a dragon, and the rise and fall of beliefs as but traces left by the four seasons.[10]

·YOU ARE COMPLETE IN YOURSELF·

We are complete in ourselves. There is no creator, there is no creation, and there is only Life. Life flows through us and we participate in that life being open to God and transparent to life. Everything is enlightened for everything we look on is enlightened. Our affirming of the whole of life leads us to that truth and that experience. There is nothing for us to do but participate and the only principle is that Love is all.

Differentiating between aspects of divinity, rather than feeling compassion towards the All is the source of our unhappiness. Swami Vivekananda observed:

> Behind everything the same divinity is existing, and out of this comes the basis of morality... Love everyone as your own self, because the whole universe is one... this little personalized self is the cause of all my misery. This individualized self, which makes me different from all other beings, brings hatred and jealousy and misery, struggle and all other evils... So this is to be given up. We must always hold ourselves ready, even to give up our lives for the lowest beings.[11]

Only by being compassionate to the All can we make the ultimate step to freedom by *becoming* compassion.

> One afternoon, I was waiting outside school to pick up my children. I watched as the parents greeted their children. I saw how each child was the focus of love for their particular parent and how each child was preferred and favoured. I began to wonder about the preference I have for my own children. I thought, 'I am sitting here while children are starving, dying and being hurt in a million different ways. Why does it not affect me?'
>
> Love is not a partial thing. It is so easy just loving what is easy to love. There

was something in me that wanted to love beyond the biological and psychological limitations of being a parent.

This is an intimation of transcendent love. It is only by surpassing the emotional chains of individual love that we connect to all things. The enlightened life is not separate but connected. We are that part of Life that is self-aware, conscious, and transcendent.

If you have a preference and if you live within the limitation of that preference and do not aspire beyond it, then you are in that place where, 'I see the world as I am.' Yet your true heart is not going to be satisfied with anything less than everything, until you ask yourself, 'How can I love whatever is before me?' How do you get to the place where you could really love the whole world, love everything, love Life in all of its forms? Love offers everything and withholds nothing.

All life is sacred and it is only the clinging to the small separate self that distances us from anybody, or anything, else. Sometimes the unexpected occurs and, if we can leave the self on the sidelines, truth, compassion and oneness with all life simply flow within us:

One day, two policeman were driving up the Pali road when they saw, just beyond the railings that keeps the cars from rolling over, a young man preparing to jump. The police car stopped, and the policeman on the right jumped out to grab the man but caught him just as he jumped, and he was himself being pulled over when the second officer arrived just in time to pull the two of them back.

Do you realize what had suddenly happened to that policeman who had given himself to death with that unknown youth? Everything else in his life had dropped off – his duty to his family, his duty to his job, his duty to his own life – all of his wishes and hopes for his lifetime had just disappeared. He was about to die.

Later, a newspaper reporter asked him, 'Why didn't you let go? You would have been killed.' And his reported answer was, 'I couldn't let go. If I had let that young man go, I couldn't have lived another day of my life.'[12]

The policeman had flipped into unified Consciousness. When he acted so purely and so unselfconsciously, all the personal concerns of his life were put aside and he acted as if the threat to the young man's life was a threat to his own. At that moment he was living Vivekananda's words, 'Love everyone as your own self, because the whole universe is one.' He had entered the spiritual path of Thou and I – of pure service – when he spontaneously offered up his life to save the life of another. His life and the young man's life were the same life.

• NOTHING MATTERS •

One of the deepest spiritual truths, and one of the most challenging and liberating, is that nothing matters. Without this truth we are powerless to love anything and incapable of becoming transparent to Love. Even while we are doing the things that we need to do and taking it all perfectly seriously, we know that none of it matters.

Nothing matters because everything is Love and we fulfil that by allowing love through us. If something matters, then something matters *more* than something else; somebody is *more* lovable than somebody else; this flower is *better* than that flower; and certain aspects of existence are *better* than others. Nothing matters is the reflection of everything matters: you cannot have one without the other. There is no creator and no creation, just dancing with Life without judgement, in pure awareness. No thing matters. This life is really the passing play of *samsara*.

Thus shall ye think of all this fleeting world, a star at dawn, a bubble in a stream, a child's laugh, a phantasm, a dream.

• ACCEPTANCE AND FORGIVENESS •

The practice of deep acceptance and total forgiveness are integral to the spiritual life. When we approach everybody in this way our beings blossom and our lives are transformed. Work with forgiveness, because not forgiving closes the heart, reduces love and compassion, and increases fear and contraction.

Many years ago, I was invited to attend the blessing ceremony of the baby of some friends. I wanted to give something, so I meditated deeply on the themes of purity and innocence. I was wondering how we could offer pure love to this new life when the theme of forgiveness emerged. Some words came and I developed them into a song.

The ceremony took place in a beautiful garden at the height of summer. Some of us decided to improvise a ritual. We arranged everybody in a circle around the baby and asked everyone to turn and face the person next to him or her. I sang a verse of the song and then they would sing the chorus to each other and pass on to the next person in the circle. The words of the chorus were:

> I forgive you,
> You forgive me.
> The Love within us
> Bless the baby.

Afterwards, as we were all standing around together, I overheard some people speaking about the ceremony. In heated voices they said, 'Why did we have to sing I forgive you and you forgive me? What has that got to do with a baby blessing ceremony?'

We are oblivious to the depth of our blame, resentment, and unwillingness to forgive. We are offended at the suggestion that we are harbouring thoughts of vengeance for what has been done to us. This is the strength of the stranglehold that victim-consciousness has on our lives. We should all persistently practise acceptance and forgiveness in everyday life. Persistent forgiveness is like water wearing away stone.

· LOOK AT YOURSELF ·

Seeing, responding and working openly with yourself and your veils and illusions are essential practices. Practise constant self-awareness until the self is no more.

'First, before you start serving anybody else, be absolutely selfish. How can you serve anybody else unless you have attained your inner being first? Be absolutely selfish!'... To be absolutely selfish does not mean to be uncontrollably selfish but to be Selfish, to fulfil one's own spiritual destiny, which is to realize God.[13]

There are two ways to work with the deep urges of desire in the small self. Either, we settle down to penetrate deeply to the root and sever it there, or, we follow the urges with awareness, until we have seen through the illusion of separation that they represent. We are then free to follow desire without the taint of illusion.

Begin by removing judgement and allow yourself what you desire without hindrance or criticism. You may need a period in your life in which you are courageous enough to go after everything you want. When you are ready and you have the courage, practise pure selfishness, as the fulfilment of the Self. Everything can be offered to God when the selfishness has been realized in the Self. We are responsible for where we direct our passion and desire. The philosopher Martin Buber wrote:

One should not kill 'the evil impulse', the passion, in oneself, but one shall serve God with it; it is the power, which is destined to receive its direction from man.[14]

• GOD WILL DISAPPEAR AND YOU WILL REMAIN •

Among the many seductions on the spiritual path, the Zen Buddhists identify 'gedo' Zen, the practice of Zen to gain supernatural powers and visions. Examples of this are Christian contemplation and the miracles of Jesus. 'Gedo' Zen is considered a place of fascination that you should not get stuck in. William Johnston recounts the following conversation with a Zen Roshi:

Roshi: Tell me, what about your Zen? What are you doing?
Johnston: I'm doing what you, I suppose, would call 'gedo' Zen.
Roshi: Very good! Very good! Many Christians do that. But what precisely do you mean by 'gedo Zen'?

Johnston: I mean that I am sitting silently in the presence of God without words or thoughts or images or ideas.

Roshi: Your God is everywhere?

Johnston: Yes.

Roshi: And you are wrapped around in God?

Johnston: Yes.

Roshi: And you experience this.

Johnston: Yes.

Roshi: Very good! Very good! Just continue this way. Just keep on. And eventually you will find that God will disappear and only Johnston San will remain. This remark shocked me... I said with a smile, 'God will not disappear. But Johnston might well disappear and only God will be left'.

'Yes, yes', he answered smilingly. 'It's the same thing. That is what I mean.'[15]

As soon as the mind forms the thought, 'I am sitting silently in the presence of God without words or thoughts or images or ideas', the reality of it is lost. The experience is substituted by the thought and the thought separates us from the experience. The mind is so wily that even the thought, 'I have no thought', is enough to separate us. The tiniest, single thought is enough to prevent you entering the doorway to heaven. However slight your denial of the whole, you remain in separation. The Zen Patriarch Dogen wrote:

> ... the separation will be as that between heaven and earth if even the slight-est gap exists...[16]

One single thought, one single attachment, one tiny clinging, one tiny aspect of the small self, one resentment, one act of un-forgiveness, one desire still yearned for, one corner of the unconscious unlit, one single idea, one single image – any one of these is enough for the illusion to be total.

Letting go of the very last thing, the final constraint on consciousness, is slipping over the wall, jumping into the abyss, taking that fork in the road marked 'unknown'.

The Self arises to fill, fulfil, and go beyond our petty lives. The Self is the God that is 'wrapped around us'. The Self is I, the Self is You, and the Self is All. Atman is Brahman – the individual soul is the absolute Soul. Your centre

is the Axis Mundi. The world before you is the whole world. The eyes you look into are Brahman, as are the eyes that look back at you. There is no mirror any more and so there is no projection.
There is no hiding any more and so there are no secrets and no shame. The love and the wisdom inside you is Love, is Wisdom, is the Absolute. That Thou Art. We were always here.

Freedom consists in the spontaneous activity of the total, integrated personality...

Erich Fromm

'Your God is everywhere' – in the eyes of your enemy as well as your friend, on a dark depressing day as well as a bright, happy one, in your failures as well as your successes, in the ugly and the beautiful. God – the Self – is there and always the same, whatever the conditions.

In his small ground-floor apartment in the slums of Bombay, where he lived with his wife and four children, the realized master Nisargadatta announced to devotees and pilgrims:

There is no question of going anywhere, arriving anywhere, or doing anything; you are already there.[17]

· SILENCE ·

For three years we had trained together. We had witnessed each other's fears, anger and needs. We had sat with each other's pain. We had shared each other's lives, from dramas to insights, and touched each other's realities. Not one of us had failed to grow over all that time. Now, finally, it was the last session of the last day. Between coffee-time and our last lunch together, we would finally end and this group would never meet again. The room was thick with the distant echoes of our experiences, together and apart. Over those years, the group had always been a touchstone, an accepting confidant, a zone of safety and acceptance. We sat in a circle, each one of us waiting for someone to speak. Slowly, slowly, as the time ticked on, our expectancy deepened into a profound silence. Not ordinary silence, but the silence of great intimacy. After all the words, we had arrived at the place where there was nothing left to say, where we could simply come together and be.

To seek freedom is the only driving force I know. Freedom to fly off into infinity. Freedom to dissolve; to lift off; to be like the flame of a candle, which, in spite of being up against the light of a billion stars, remains intact, because it never pretended to be more than what it is: a mere candle.

Don Juan

To realize the Eternal in everyday life, to manifest the divine in the human realm, effort is futile and seeking takes us further away. In the silence between words, in pauses, in the willingness to wait and finally in silence, consciousness flies. The Eternal finds its deepest expression in profound silence. Like the breath inside the breath, the God inside the man or woman, the sound of one hand clapping, the answer to the question, 'Who am I?' the name of God is uttered in sacred silence. This silence is within and eternal. This still-point is the true Self, our real centre. We can act from this place at any time; we can practise from this place. This is the heart centre – the Self.

In Ramana Maharshi's ashram this was the practice of *darshan*, the deepest meeting possible:

> One could not sit there for long without becoming aware that this silence was not mere absence of sound but a positive spiritual influence, even a spiritual force. It was as though a light breeze blew down the hall, or as though a stream flowed through it, a stream of purity, and this breeze, this stream, seemed to emanate from the silent, nodding figure on the couch, who did nothing in particular, only reading the letters that were brought to him or glancing, every now and then, at some member of the congregation with keen but kindly eye. Sitting there in the hall... I felt the stream flow over me, felt it flow over body and mind, over thoughts and emotions, until body, mind, thoughts and emotions had all been washed away, and there remained nothing but a great shining peace.[18]

Silence is the resonant void, the place of all potential, of all creation; the place where you awake from a dream of death, laughing out loud, because you know that death and life are the same. There is nowhere to go, nothing to do, nothing but 'what is'. Silence is the perfect teaching, the purest expression of the absolute nature of being. Finally, we are at one with the True Self and know that we were never separate. We are never without the celestial sound of the 'silent music'.

> You discover in the silence that you are loved, that you are lovable. It is the discovery that everyone must make in their lives if they are going to become fully themselves, fully human.[19]

·THE FLIGHT OF CONSCIOUSNESS·

At the end of the journey we find ourselves in the place where we started. But we are now fully present with no distinction between human and divine, inner and outer, self and other. To be divine is to be fully human and to be fully human is itself divine.

When I was young, I dipped into a book that had colour plates of the microscopic worlds of creatures that were too small to be seen by the naked eye. It showed me a universe of bizarre, alien beings that lived on my skin, in my hair and in my internal organs. I understood then that my perception depended on my position; where I was seeing it from shaped what it looked like. Later on I realized that if I became fixed in my view, I could never find the truth and if I never found the truth, I could never be free.

If there is a universe in a hair follicle, a grain of sand, or a raindrop, then each universe fully realized is the realization of all universes. When I am aware, the world is aware; when I forgive, the world forgives; when I am the Self, the world is the Self. This is so for negative projections – how much more so for spiritual reality.

Every moment is a *bardo* state – a portal of change, an opening. A breath is the portal, or a thought, a gesture, a letting go, a cry, a leaf falling from a tree, a ripple in the lake – anything. Consciousness flies in both macrocosm and microcosm alike. I gaze at the horizon and see Krishna of the Gita at the dawning of individual consciousness; Lao Tzu with his rich observations of the Way; Buddha teaching the ultimate doctrine of mind; Jesus as the living example of total forgiveness – each path transcendent of its individual taste and inflection and complete in itself – and in our time, the realization of the Higher Self in the merging of individuality and spirituality. What is to follow? OurSelf?

This single *bardo* moment holds the key now. The spiritual individual, the Self, deepens in unity, resonates with the suffering and the joy of others and makes it her own,

takes one step and it is all,
utters one word and it is all,
loves and Love is All.
There is no saviour,
the world waits for no one
but You
and as soon as you take one step on the path with sincerity,
You are here
You are
You.

EXERCISES FOR THE TEN STAGES

Some of the exercises can be done alone, others in a group, and most of them can be adapted to either way of working. Remember that inner work is essentially a solo process anyway. Do not feel that you have to do all of these exercises or that you have to do them in any particular order. Select the ones that 'feel right' for you.

You will need paper and pens, a drawing pad (large is best!) and some coloured pencils, crayons or paints to express yourself creatively, a quiet space to work in, a notebook (possibly a few) plus your openness, curiosity and serious intent.

Do not forget to give yourself acknowledgement and praise for your inner work. This is crucially important since no one can ever really know and appreciate what you have done – other than you. Praising yourself is a stimulus that encourages you to return enthusiastically to your work the next time.

Enjoy spending time with yourself. Create a beautiful and peaceful environment for your inner work and never lose sight of your spiritual destination, which is wholeness, love, and wisdom.

Before you begin, try answering these questions:

Your Spiritual Path
Where are you on your spiritual path?

Questions
What are your spiritual questions?

The Present
What are your present issues, concerns, and dissatisfactions?

Your Life Lessons
What are your life lessons?

STAGE 1: SEEING YOURSELF AS YOU ARE

Sitting Meditation

In sitting meditation the aim is simply to sit. Your back should be straight, but not rigid; your body relaxed, comfortable and balanced. You should have a firm and grounded base (the lotus, the half lotus, or an open cross-legged posture is good, as is kneeling using a meditation stool. If sitting on the floor is a problem sit to the front of a chair with your feet flat on the floor). Your hands should be relaxed and held gently in your lap and you should breathe normally. Watch your thoughts come and go and simply be a witness to them. Be patient when you wander off in your mind and gently, but firmly, bring yourself back to sitting.

Lifeline

Draw a line on a large piece of paper. The line can be whatever shape you like. The line represents your life from birth to the present day. Now draw, or write in, significant people, places, and events along the line in the appropriate place using form and colour. If possible, do this exercise with a friend, or in a group, and talk through your lifelines when you have finished.

Life Story

Tell your life story in the third person, either to a friend or into a tape recorder (and play it back later). Here are two variations on this exercise: give yourself a short amount of time – say fifteen minutes or less – so that you have to be very selective; choose a particular period of your life.

Your Autobiography

Write an autobiography of the first 21 years of your life in three chapters of 7 years each. Use these key areas to stimulate your thoughts: significant events, where you lived, God and the spiritual, Nature, play, experiences of the senses, your family, school and religion, emotional life, other people, ideas and influences.

Fairy Story

Write a fairy story about a child. The child is you. Represent the elements of your childhood by symbols – castles, mountains, rivers, woods, kings and queens, witches, dwarves, elves, dragons. The story line should aim to resolve your early childhood needs.

Self Image

Write down 3 things that you think other people would say are good and bad about you. Then write down 3 things you think are good and bad about you. Compare the two lists.

Intimacy

Draw a picture entitled 'Intimacy'.

Good and Bad

Write two lists: one headed 'bad', the other 'good'. Try not to think about it too much — simply write — then review the lists and consider what you have learned about yourself.

Where Am I Now?

A friend can read out this guided imagery or you can tape it and play it back to yourself. Find somewhere where you will not be interrupted and be comfortable and relaxed. The words should be read slowly, with long breaks between the phrases in a measured tone and a consistent rhythm. Allow enough time for the images to form. Don't rush the process! Allow at least 15 minutes of quiet time after the words finish.

> You are lost in a dark forest... you feel afraid and you want to get out so much that you begin to tear about in all directions... you are repeatedly convinced that this way is the way out... and that way is the way out... and another way appears... and then another... and another... until you become further lost. Your fear increases to terror and you are becoming exhausted... finally you collapse in a heap and slowly you begin to notice a dim light through the trees. Over a period of time you patiently track the light... and realize that it is re-orientating you. You climb the nearest tall tree and look about noticing landmarks... you rest a while... you wait... tracking the light... taking in your surroundings... then... when you are sure... you take the first step out of the dark wood towards the light.

I'm Proud of...

Take a piece of paper and write at the top, 'I'm proud of...' then write a list — without thinking too much. What do you think of what you wrote? How does it make you feel?

Who Am I?

Throughout the day, behind all your activity, keep this question constantly in your awareness.

The Gift

Think of something you would like to give to someone you love... then give it to yourself.

Old and New Models

Make two lists, one headed 'old models', the other 'new models.' The old models come from your conditioning, so they fulfil what you habitually expect from life. The new models are the ones you aspire to.

What Am I Carrying?

Select one thing that you are carrying which you do not need. Make a promise to yourself to let it go and write down a statement of your intention. For example, you might select guilt, resentment, anger, worthlessness and so on.

STAGE 2: DEVELOPING FAITH

After Your Death

Meditate on 'The Day After My Death' for 20-30 minutes. Write down, and discuss if possible, what you discover.

Your Death

Draw a picture entitled 'My Death'.

The Five Senses

List the five senses in order of their importance to you. List your likes and dislikes for each of the five senses. Draw pictures entitled, ' touching', 'hearing', 'seeing', 'tasting', and 'smelling'.

Divine Signs

How did you begin your spiritual journey? Make a drawing of your 'sign', or how you discovered 'the footprints' of the Divine. Draw pictures of the enlightening experiences and the spiritual insights you have had.

Innocence

Draw a picture entitled 'Innocence'.

Vipassana Meditation

Sit in a comfortable position – as in Sitting Meditation in Stage 1 – and follow the breath in and out. Fix your attention on the point on your nose where the breath enters the nostrils. Whenever you become distracted, return your attention there. As thoughts and sensations arise, simply let them go and continue to follow your breath.

Spiritual Journal

Record your spiritual journey in a journal. Spend some time bringing it up-to-date. Make the commitment to keep an ongoing record. You could include spiritual experiences, insights, understanding, visions, dreams, synchronous events, inner wisdom and guidance, poems (your own and others'), drawings and inspiring passages.

Disappointment, Disillusionment, Disenchantment

Can you recall an experience of disappointment, disillusionment or disenchantment that deepened you? Reflect on it then honour it through writing, drawing or ritual.

Innocence, Imagination, Creativity

How was your innocence denied and your imagination devalued? How was your creativity stunted?

Early Criticism

What criticisms did you receive in your early life? Who criticized you? How did you feel? What impact has criticism had on you?

Healing Illness

Record your experiences of healing illness, as a child or as an adult. Often illness is a way for the deep unconscious to communicate to us. Illness can be a passage to spiritual insight and transformation. Look back and consider your experiences of illness in the light of this.

I Am Not…

This exercise invites and acknowledges your shadow. List your defining qualities under the heading, 'I am not…' For instance, if you consider yourself kind, write, 'I am not kind'. When you have completed your list, read it through, be aware of your feelings, and explore the truth of the reversed statements.

STAGE 3: AWARENESS

Walking Meditation

Just walk, slowly with awareness. Your eyes may be open or closed. Feel your footsteps, the weight of your body, the breath in your body, and how you are balanced. Be at one with the walking and let go of thought. Let your arms hang loosely at your sides, let your body be open and, when your mind becomes distracted, gently bring yourself back to simply walking.

Resolving Unfinished Business

Write a list of all the people in your life, living or dead, and all the situations, present or past, in which you have lost your energy and which remain unresolved in some way. All of these relationships and situations need to be resolved so you can be all that you are. Write letters to the people with whom you have unfinished business (it is not necessary to send them), start an inner dialogue with them (it is useful to record this so you can look over it), visualize them sitting in front of you (you can use a cushion for this), and talk through your issues with them. What do you need to do to reach resolution?

Where I Am...

Write a list entitled 'Where I am...' under 9 headings. The 9 headings are: historically, emotionally, in relationships (include yourself), creatively/artistically, mentally/intellectually, physically/energetically, professionally (career/occupation), financially, and spiritually. Be truthful and honest. This exercise can help you to get to know yourself better. Appreciate yourself for those areas in which you are fulfilled. Ask yourself what you can do about the areas that are lacking.

The 'Knower'

Ask yourself: What do I pretend not to know and avoid taking responsibility for?

Blind Walk

Go on a 'blind walk' with a friend. Close your eyes and let your friend lead you. After about thirty minutes, swap roles. The whole exercise should be done with no verbal communication. When you are leading, give your friend opportunities to experience without 'labelling'. For example, you could put a stick of wood in their hands, brush grass on their cheek, lead them by a field of lavender, let them hear animals moving or children playing.

All-inclusive Awareness

Go to a place you are attracted to and remain there – perhaps for an hour. Just sit, lie, or stand and take in the environment with all your senses and awareness. Include everything; exclude nothing. Be open to the experience and do not be limited by your models of experience. Allow your being to merge with this place.

Choicelessness

Practise choiceless awareness by being non-discriminatory. Some examples are reading whatever comes to hand, eating whatever is available, sitting wherever is offered, or interacting with people without following your usual preferences. Notice what happens inside you when you discard the habits and judgements of your small self.

Drama and Beyond

You need 3 pieces of paper bound together down one side. Draw a picture of 'the drama' of your life. When you have finished, cut a way through your picture and draw another picture called 'the witness' on the page underneath. When you have finished, cut a way through that picture and draw a third picture called 'beyond'.

Awareness

Write a poem entitled 'Awareness'.

STAGE 4: LESSENING

Letting Go

Meditate on everything you cling to, on everything you believe you are, and practise letting go. Sit as previously described in Sitting Meditation in Stage 1. As thoughts and images appear, simply watch and let go. You may be surprised to find that they pass and, as they pass, new thoughts and images come into being. Simply continue watching and letting go for 20-30 minutes.

Letting Go Of What You Believe You Are

Either write down, or share with a partner, all you believe you are – your body, your mind, your experiences, your achievements, your faults, your virtues, and so on. As you express each belief, take a breath... as you breathe out, let go of it.

EXERCISES

Deflated Ego

Write a short autobiographical story about your ego being deflated. What did you learn ?

Re-enchantment

How do you need to become re-enchanted? Identify the areas of your life and relationship where something is missing and the enchantment is gone. How could you get it back?

A Ritual

Ritualize an event in your life that you have gone through, or are going through, which has lessened you. Ritual is the outward acknowledgement of an inner process. It bridges the inner and outer by connecting the spiritual and the material. Whatever you enact as ritual – from the simple act of lighting of a candle to an elaborate group event – should be done with awareness and reverence.

Dialoguing Between the self and the Self

Write a spontaneous dialogue between your small self and the Higher Self.

Life Lessons

What are your life lessons? Consider what life is trying to teach you through the lessons it presents you with. What are the themes? Consider your life lessons on three levels. First, the lesson of your whole life; second, the lesson you are learning in this period of your life and, third, the part of the lesson you are working with now.

Resolving the Past

Think of a scenario from the past, which continues to concern or disturb you. Role-play the scenario with others, then each share what the experience was like. What feelings were evoked? Why are you attached to this scenario? Record what you have learnt and work towards resolution and letting go.

Attraction/Repulsion

What attracts you? What repulses you? Write down in detail the qualities, the things, the people, and the places that you find attractive and repulsive.

Ideal Partner

Describe your ideal partner in writing or drawing.

STAGE 5: OPENING

Life Statements

Draw the outline of a tree on a large piece of paper and write your core life statement along the trunk, your major life statements along the main branches, and your minor life statements along the smaller branches. For example, your core life statement might be 'I am worthless', your major life statements might be 'I am not good enough' and 'Nobody likes me' and your minor life statements might be 'Nobody wants to hear what I have to say' and 'I never get what I want'. Keep an ongoing record of your life statements on your tree, as you become aware of them.

Practise Opening

Pick somebody who you are having difficulty with. Notice how you get into conflict. Now, place him or her in your heart and practise opening.

I Am Afraid of...

Write, 'I am afraid of…' at the top of a piece of paper and let your hand write in the endings – without thinking too much. Are there any surprises?

Adventure Story

Write an adventure story in which the hero or heroine is victorious through trust and innocence.

Retrieving Your Energy

With a group of friends, role-play a scenario from your past where your energy got caught. Choose people to act the different roles. When you have played out what actually happened, replay the scenario again with a positive outcome.

Opening Your Energy Centres

Lie on the floor and breathe. Let go of your thoughts and bring all your attention to your breath. After doing this for a few minutes, become aware of your pelvis, belly, chest, and throat and notice any tensions in these areas. Notice if there are any emotions attached to these tensions. Then direct your breath to each area in turn and, as you do, allow that area to open, release and expand. When you have finished, remain on the floor for a few minutes breathing normally and integrating the changes in your energy.

Love and Fear
In a half-hour meditation session, meditate on love for 15 minutes, then meditate on fear for 15 minutes.

A Special Friendship
Invite a special friendship into your life in which you can practise complete openness and total honesty.

STAGE 6: POWER & SURRENDER

Humming
Sit in a relaxed position (see Sitting Meditation in Stage 1) with your eyes closed. Hum loudly enough so that you feel vibrations throughout your body. Allow the pitch to alter, inhale as necessary, and allow swaying and slow movements in the body as they occur. Visualize your body as hollow and filled with the vibrations of the humming. Work with this exercise for approximately 30 minutes. Try this also with a partner, sitting comfortably opposite each other and holding hands.

Dishonesty
Take an inventory of all the ways in which you are dishonest. Include dishonesty with yourself, dishonesty with others, not saying all you mean, giving the appearance of being something you are not, lying to get what you want, and so on.

Choice
Identify issues and areas in your life where you could make more truthful and more courageous choices. What are these choices? Why do you not make them?

'Inhabiting' Emotions
As emotions arise in you, instead of pushing them away, allow yourself to be in the centre of them in a neutral way. Simply 'inhabit' them and, without your habitual reaction, watch as the feelings change and release.

Divine Longing
Draw a picture entitled 'Divine Longing'.

Goalless-ness

Whatever you are doing, wherever you are going, whatever you are trying to achieve, be present. Let the goal of your actions become a part of the process, rather than struggling to reach it. Sometimes you might be able to let go of your goal altogether and simply enjoy the moment. Write up your experiences of goalless-ness.

Adversary-helper

Adversary-helpers are those people and situations in our lives that teach us spiritual lessons. Write descriptions, draw portraits and try to role-play your adversary-helpers. If you are in a group that wants to do this, then ask someone to role-play you and explore what it is like for you to role-play your adversary-helper. Remember that adversary-helpers are not only people. They may come in the form of recurrent health problems (like migraines or back pain), attitudes (like impatience or subservience), or external events (like losing your job or having an accident). Be creative and find a way to role-play these too.

Selflessness

Perform acts of selfless giving. At first, you may have to force the acts, but, as time goes on, they will feel more natural. Let go of any attachment to the act and aim at unself-conscious giving.

Synchronicity

Note down the synchronous events of your life. Try sharing these experiences with a friend.

STAGE 7: EXPANSION

Disempowerment

How do you disempower yourself in word, thought, or action? In what particular situations do you disempower yourself? How do you disempower others?

Models of Power

Who taught you about power? How did they teach you? What are your models of power? What affect does this have on you today? Do you know the difference between having power over somebody or something, and personal power?

Centring Consciousness

Usually we centre our consciousness in our physical heads and identify ourselves with our minds. Try placing your consciousness in your chest. If you stay with this experience for just a little while, your breathing will change, your experience will change, and you will think less and feel more. Try centring your consciousness in other areas of your body and notice how this affects you.

Spiritual Reference Points

Spiritual reference points are words or phrases, stories, poems, events, or something someone did or said, which connected you with some deep understanding or insight. Reference points help you to recall important ideas. Keep a notebook of your reference points so you can remember what they refer to with vividness and clarity.

Expanding Energy

This exercise should be done in a standing position with space around you. Where do you begin and end? How big are you? One by one, become aware of your body, your physical sensations, your emotions, and your thoughts. Now become aware of the energy that surrounds you and reach out into it with your hands. Outline the space all around you with your fingertips, reaching as far as you can in all directions. Your energy field is shaped like an egg and it is a living part of your being. When you feel you have finished, simply stand with your arms at your sides for a few minutes and experience your energy.

Forgiveness Dialogue

Make a list of all the people you feel anger towards for whatever reason. These are the people you need to forgive. Work through your list one by one, exploring how you can find ways to let go of your grievances, your anger, and your revenge feelings. Try dialoguing with them – take a piece of paper and talk with them. Keep the paper to look back on. Begin to forgive in small ways. Acknowledge your reluctance, inability, or unwillingness to forgive them – but start to keep them in your heart. The first process of forgiveness may turn out to be the most difficult. Take as much time as you need, start the process now, and intend forgiveness.

If only... then...

Meditate on regrets. How would you have done it differently? What would you have done differently? What would you like to have achieved? Use the format, 'If only... then...'

Archetypal Role-play

With a group of friends, choose a myth that is important to you. Choose the character you most identify with. You will role-play that character. Now you decide who should play the other roles. Remember that myths include human beings, animals and archetypes. Take turns to explore your personal mythology.

Inner Wisdom

You can connect with your inner wisdom simply by asking and listening, but you must be available to hear the answer without pre-judging or preference. You can picture your question as a pebble thrown into a pond or as an arrow shot from a bow. If internal 'chatter' interferes with your ability to hear 'the still small voice within', spend some time in Sitting Meditation or Walking Meditation. Never doubt your inner wisdom or obscure the basic simplicity of it with your complexity. Be careful that your question does not prescribe the answer as in, 'What do I have to do about...?' You may not have to *do* anything! Keep your questions open and, if in doubt, ask, 'What do I need to know now?'

Psyche and Eros

Draw a picture of Psyche and Eros in your life. Remember Psyche represents the feminine, the human soul, the earth, and beauty. Eros represents the masculine, the god-like spirit, the heavens, and the Divine. Let your picture describe the relationship between these two aspects of yourself.

Expanding Consciousness

Experience yourself as the centre of the room you are in right now. Fill the room with your consciousness by extending it until you are occupying the entire space. Notice how this simple practice changes your awareness.

Expanding Relationships

Spend 40 minutes with your partner, spouse or friend. For 10 minutes complain, grumble and be as petty as you can about your relationship. Then spend 10 minutes expressing your deepest, most heartfelt feelings towards them. Then reverse roles.

Everything is Enlightened

Meditate on: everything is divine, everything is God's face and form, and everything is Love.

STAGE 8: ONENESS WITH THE SELF

Dance Meditation

Play some music or let there be silence, open the window to the sound of the wind or to the celestial music then... dance! If you 'can't dance' then do not call it dancing – call it moving! Let the movement be a meditation, an expression of you, a surrendering... Afterwards lie down, be still and feel the energies flowing through your body.

The Gifts of Life

Sit with your arms open, reaching out as far out as you can, as if you are embracing a great basket and all of life's gifts are falling into it. Reach out from your heart and make yourself available to receive. Hold your arms out, relax your shoulders, and relax your face. Allow the pain that you may sometimes feel around your chest, a sensation like 'rocks' in your heart, be released. Take a deep breath, feel grateful for the gifts of life, and expand.

Introduce the Other

Sit in a group circle and introduce the person to your left. Go around the circle until everyone has had a turn then share your experiences with each other.

Desire

With a group of friends, take an extra large piece of paper and draw a group picture entitled, 'Desire'.

Time for Yourself

Assess your personal need for time for yourself to be alone and find ways to achieve it. A half-hour or an hour in the day is very beneficial, as is longer periods completely away from everyday demands.

Celebration and Regrets

If your life ended now, what would you regret? What would you celebrate? What would you be grateful for?

At OM

Sit and invite a sense of belonging with nowhere to go, nothing to do, no urgency, no striving – allow yourself to be at OM.

Prayer

Each morning, soon after waking, compose a little prayer for the day and state your intent and your commitment to your spiritual unfolding.

Song

Compose a song about the beauty of life. Sing it out loud!

Resistance

Make a list of your resistances to relationship (include your relationship with yourself), to Life, and to the Self.

Filling Yourself with Light

Allow the mind to be silent and peaceful. From your inner stillness and emptiness, begin to fill yourself with love and expansiveness, positivity and beauty, abundance and light.

STAGE 9: RETURNING TO THE SOURCE

Declaration

Write a declaration of your commitment to your spiritual transformation.

Suffering and the small self

Write an essay entitled 'suffering'. Then re-write it from the point of view of the small, separate self.

Doing Good

Write two true-life accounts – one of doing good and the other of good being done to you. Look deeply into the narratives – what do you see?

Selfish and Spiritual

What desires of the small self must be met before you can realize the Self?

Notebook of Life's Teaching

Where do you get caught? Start a notebook of Life's teachings. Look for recurring themes and common triggers. What can you learn about yourself from this?

Good and Evil

Draw a beautiful picture of 'evil' and an ugly picture of 'good'.

Bliss

What does your bliss mean to you? Write it down and make a list of all your resistances.

See the World As I Am…

Relate back to yourself, by winding in your projections, everything you experience as 'out there'. Find out how much of yourself you are unwilling to own. If you see the world as you are, what would happen if you allow yourself to be as you would like the world to be?

STAGE 10: FREEDOM

Drama & Freedom

Draw a picture of the drama of life. Draw a picture entitled 'Freedom'.

Practising Invisibility

In a setting with which you are familiar, hold your energy in and notice what occurs. Does anything change? Do people treat you differently? Do you feel differently? Now let your energy out and notice the difference. This exercise should help you to gauge how much energy you expend, as well as what effect your energy has on your life.

Your Image

Describe your image in writing and drawing. Consider the function of your image. What does it do for you? How is it successful? How is it flawed (in your opinion)? Who or what have you based your image on?

Projective Relationships

Choose a person who is important in your life. Don't start with your best friend or partner – but someone who is important. Consider the kind of relationship you have. Write on a piece of paper, 'I need you, [name of person], to see my…' and fill in a list of endings.

Being Selfish

Write down and commit yourself to getting three things you want for yourself.

Affirming All Things

A fully open heart affirms all things. What prevents you from opening your heart fully? What prevents you from affirming all things? Work with these two questions until the answers are perfectly matched.

Goodness

Consider yourself as a 'good' person. What is your definition of 'good'? What constitutes a 'good' act? What is the most accomplished act of 'goodness' you have performed? Appraise your goodness.

Exercises in Truth

This exercise requires a minimum of 3 people. One of you is 'the listener', one 'the speaker', and one 'the witness'. The listener 'listens' with his whole being, opens in his energy centres, and receives the speaker while watching his own thoughts, criticisms and judgements go by. The speaker shares whatever is going on for him in the moment, allowing spontaneity and intending truth. Finally, the witness witnesses in the purest sense, while letting go of judgements and reactions. The roles should be rotated twice, so that each person takes a turn in each role. Finally, there is a sharing session where each of you reflects on how you experienced each role.

Gazing

Sit opposite a friend (or in front of a large mirror) and make eye contact. Watch what happens – both inside and out – breathe easily, relax into the experience. When you feel finished, close your eyes and be with yourself.

A Letter from the Enlightened Self

Write a letter to yourself from your enlightened Self. Give it to a friend to keep for a while and post to you after a lapse of time.

The Group

Form a group of people who are on the spiritual journey. Spend time together sitting in silence, talking about your lives and encouraging each other's spiritual development. Exchange time in pairs – as sharers and listeners – and do exercises for the ten stages together.

Suggested Reading

STAGE 1: SEEING YOURSELF AS YOU ARE

Zen Flesh, Zen Bones, Paul Reps, Pelican 1978
A Flower Does Not Talk, Abbot Zenkei Shibayama, Tuttle 1993
The Art of Storytelling, Nancy Mellon, Element 1992
The Teachings of Ramana Maharshi, ed. Arthur Osborne, Century 1987
Hakomi Therapy, Ron Kurtz, Hakomi Institute 1983

STAGE 2: DEVELOPING FAITH

Emotional Anatomy, Stanley Keleman, Center 1985
The Hero with a Thousand Faces, Joseph Campbell, Paladin 1988
Focusing, Eugene Gendlin, Bantam 1981
Shobogenzo, Dogen Zenji, University of Hawaii Press (USA) 1986
Realms of the Human Unconscious, Stanislav Grof, Viking 1975

STAGE 3: AWARENESS

How Can I Help? Ram Dass and Paul Gorman, Knopf 1993
A Gradual Awakening, Stephen Levine, Century 1989
The Knee of Listening, Da Free John, Dawn Horse Press 1988
Gestalt Therapy, Friedrich S. Perls, Ralph Hefferline and Paul Goodman,
Gestalt Journal Press (USA) 1996
Duino Elegies, Rainer Maria Rilke, trans. David Young, Norton 1978
Awakening the Heart, ed. John Welwood, New Science Library 1983

STAGE 4: LESSENING

A Guide to the I Ching, Carol A. Anthony, Anthony Publishing 1988
I Ching, Richard Wilhelm, Routledge & Kegan Paul 1951

In Search of the Miraculous, P.D.Ouspensky, Routledge & Kegan Paul 1950
Be As You Are – The Teachings of Sri Ramana Maharshi, ed. David Godman, Arkana 1985

STAGE 5: OPENING

Who Dies? Stephen Levine, Gateway Books 1988
Ecstasy, Robert A. Johnson, Harper & Row 1987
Siddhartha, Hermann Hesse, Picador 1973
On the Way to the Wedding, Linda Schierse Leonard, Shambhala 1986

STAGE 6: POWER & SURRENDER

The Wisdom of Insecurity, Alan Watts, Rider 1979
Tao Te Ching, Lao Tzu, trans. Richard Wilhelm, Arkana 1985
The Fire From Within, Carlos Castaneda, Black Swan 1985
TAO: The Watercourse Way,
Alan Watts with the collaboration of Al Chung-Liang Huang, Penguin 1979
The Courage To Be, Paul Tillich, Fontana 1962

STAGE 7: EXPANSION

The Gospel of Peace of Jesus Christ, St. John,
trans. Edmond Szekely and Purcell Weaver, C.W.Daniel Co. Ltd. 1986
The Power of Myth, Joseph Campbell, Doubleday 1988
Goddesses in Everywoman, Jean Shinoda Bolen, Harper Colophon 1985
He – Understanding Masculine Psychology, Robert A. Johnson, Harper & Row 1974
Journey of the Heart, John Welwood, Mandala 1991

STAGE 8: ONENESS WITH THE SELF

Dark Night of the Soul, St. John of the Cross, Burns & Oates 1976
Peace is Every Step, Thich Nhat Hanh, Bantam 1992
Four Quartets, T.S.Eliot, Faber and Faber 1943
The Bhagavad Gita, trans. Juan Mascaro, Penguin 1962
Memories, Dreams, Reflections, C.G.Jung, Fontana 1983

STAGE 9: RETURNING TO THE SOURCE

The Inner World of Choice, Frances G. Wickes, Sigo Press 1988
The Mythic Image, Joseph Campbell, Princeton/Bollingen 1981
Anatomy of the Spirit, Caroline Myss, Bantam 1997
Descent to the Goddess, Sylvia Brinton Perera, Inner City Books 1981
Beyond Therapy, ed. Guy Claxton, Wisdom Publications 1986

STAGE 10: FREEDOM

The Way of Chuang Tzu, Thomas Merton, New Directions 1965
Eleutherios, Da Free John, Dawn Horse Press 1998
Zen Mind, Beginner's Mind, Shunryu Suzuki, Weatherhill 1986
How to Grow a Lotus Blossom, Roshi Jiyu Kennett, Shasta Abbey 1977
Holy Madness, Georg Feuerstein, Arkana 1990
The Upanishads, trans. Juan Mascaro, Penguin 1971

NOTES TO THE TEXT

PREFACE

(1) Yogavasishtha quoted in *The Spirit of the Upanishads*, The Yogi Publication Society 1907, p.1.

STAGE 1: SEEING YOURSELF AS YOU ARE

(1) Irina Tweedie quoted in Llewellyn Vaughan-Lee, *The Call and the Echo*, Threshold Books/The Golden Sufi Order 1992, p.5; sourced from 'Sufi spiritual training is a process of individuation leading to the Infinite,' in *Sufism, Islam and Jungian Psychology*, ed. Marvin Spiegelman, pp.127-8.

(2) Ram Dass and Paul Gorman, *How Can I Help?* Alfred A. Knopf, Inc., 1985, pp. 7-8.

(3) This classic Zen story is widely related in slightly different versions. You can read it in *Zen Flesh, Zen Bones*, Compiled by Paul Reps, Penguin 1971, p.17 and *A Flower Does Not Talk – Zen Essays*, Abbot Zenkei Shibayama, Tuttle 1970, p.171. In connection with Nan-in's teaching the following is of interest: '...from the point of view of the disciple the grace of the guru is like an ocean. If he comes with a cup he will only get a cupful. It is no use complaining of the niggardliness of the ocean; the bigger the vessel the more he will be able to carry. It is entirely up to him.' – Ramana Maharshi, *Ramana Maharshi and the Path of Self Knowledge*, ed. Arthur Osborne, Samuel Weiser Inc. 1970, p.142.

(4) 'A suitcase full of dust' in *Love Poems*, Brian Patten, Flamingo 1992, p.34.

(5) Rainer Maria Rilke quoted in *Words of Wisdom*, ed. H. Exley, Exley Publications 1997.

(6) Stephen Levine, *A Gradual Awakening*, Rider 1980, p.38.

STAGE 2: DEVELOPING FAITH

(1) 'In the twelfth century the Chinese master Kakuan drew the pictures of the ten bulls, basing them on earlier Taoist bulls, and wrote the comments in prose and verse... The ten bulls represent sequent steps in the realization of one's true nature... It is a revelation of spiritual unfoldment, paralleled in every bible of human experience.' – *Zen Flesh, Zen Bones*, Compiled by Paul Reps, Pelican 1971, pp. 135-6.

(2) *The Bhagavad Gita 2.14*, trans. Juan Mascaro, Penguin 1962, p.49.

(3) St. John of the Cross, *Dark Night of the Soul*, Burns & Oates 1935, p.28.

(4) In *Be As You Are: The Teachings of Sri Ramana Maharshi*, ed. David Godman, Arkana 1985, p.157: '*Turiya* literally means the fourth state, the supreme consciousness, as distinct from the other three states: waking, dreaming and dreamless sleep. The fourth state is eternal and the other three states come and go in it.'

(5) Rumi, *Whoever Brought Me Here Will Have To Take Me Home*, trans. Coleman Barks with John Moyne, Arkana 1998, p.129-130.

(6) Swami Vivekananda, from an uncompleted book called, *The Message of Divine Wisdom*, quoted in Marcus Toyne, *Involved in Mankind: The Life and Message of Vivekananda*, Ramakrishna Vedanta Centre 1983.

(7) Richard Bach, *Illusions – The Adventures of a Reluctant Messiah*, Pan Books 1978, pp.14-17.

(8) 'The Scripture of Great Wisdom' in Roshi Jiyu Kennett, *Zen is Eternal Life*, Dharma Publishing 1976, p.277.

(9) Lao Tzu, *Tao Te Ching*, trans. D.C.Lau, Penguin Books 1963, VI, p.62.

(10) Roshi Jiyu Kennett, *How To Grow a Lotus Blossom*, Shasta Abbey 1977, p.174.

(11) Thich Nhat Hanh, *A Guide to Walking Meditation*, Fellowship Publ. 1985, p.25.

(12) Joseph Campbell, *This business of the gods...*, in conversation with Fraser Boa, Windrose Films Ltd.1989, pp.106-7.

(13) Lao Tzu, *Tao Te Ching*, trans. Dr. John C.H.Wu, ed. Dr. Paul K.T.Sih, St. John's University Press: New York 1961, chapter 13, p.17.

STAGE 3: AWARENESS

(1) The Vigyan Bhairava Tantra, the Sochanda Tantra and the Malini Vijaya Tantra – see 'Centreing' in *Zen Flesh, Zen Bones*, Compiled by Paul Reps, Pelican 1971, pp. 149-163.

(2) *Ibid.*, p.140.

(3) Ramana Maharshi, *Be As You Are: The Teachings of Sri Ramana Maharshi*, ed. David Godman, Arkana 1985, pp.11-12.

(4) See particularly P.D.Ouspensky, *In Search of the Miraculous*, Routledge and Kegan Paul 1950.

(5) From the television programme, '*Did You Used To Be R.D.Laing?*' broadcast by Channel 4 in 1989.

(6) Anthony de Mello, *Awareness*, Doubleday and Co. Inc. 1990.

(7) 'Vedanta and Privilege' in Swami Vivekananda, *The Complete Works of Swami Vivekananda*, Advaita Ashram 1984, p.422.

(8) Alan Watts, *The Wisdom of Insecurity*, Rider 1983.

(9) *Zen Flesh, Zen Bones*, compiled by Paul Reps, Pelican 1971, p.165.

STAGE 4: LESSENING

(1) *The Bhagavad Gita 2.16*, trans. Juan Mascaro, Penguin 1962, p.49.

(2) 'People today feel that their lives are without meaning. One encounters this all over the place and that's a consequence of having climbed the ladder against the wrong wall.' – Joseph Campbell, *This business of the gods...*, in conversation with Fraser Boa, Windrose Films Ltd.1989, p.21.

(3) 'Ashes present a great diminishment. If the man doesn't experience that diminishment sharply, he will retain his inflation, and continue to identify himself with all in him that can fly: his sexual drive, his mind, his refusal to commit himself, his addiction, his transcendence, his coolness.' – Robert Bly, *Iron John – A Book About Men*, Addison-Wesley Publishing Company, Inc. 1990, p.83.

(4) *Zen Lessons: the Art of Leadership*, ed. Thomas Cleary, Shambhala Publications 1991, 92, p.58. This passage echoes the words of Lord Krishna in the *Bhagavad Gita 2.15*: 'The man whom these [opposites] cannot move, whose soul is one, beyond pleasure and pain, is worthy of life in Eternity.'

(5) Jacques Lusseyran, *And There Was Light*, Heinemann 1963, p.131.

(6) From the 'Brihad-Aranyaka Upanishad' in *The Upanishads*, trans. Juan Mascaro, Penguin 1971, pp.130-131.

(7) Kabir, *The Kabir Book*, version by Robert Bly, Beacon Press 1977.

(8) P.D.Ouspensky, *The Fourth Way*, Routledge & Kegan Paul Ltd. 1977, p.35.

(9) Stephen Levine, *A Gradual Awakening*, Rider 1980, p. 52 (my italics).

(10) The animus is the masculine aspect of a woman's unconscious, as the anima is the feminine aspect of a man's unconscious. For an explanation of Jung's concepts see *The Portable Jung*, ed. Joseph Campbell, Penguin 1976, particularly 'Aion: Phenomenology of the Self', pp.139-162.

(11) "... the patripsych comes from 'the internal constellation of patriarchal patterns... By this we mean all the attitudes, ideas and feelings usually compulsive and unconscious that develop in relation to authority and control...'" – John Rowan quoting from Southgate and Randall's *The Barefoot Psychoanalyst* in *Subpersonalities*, John Rowan, p.22.

(12) Sylvia Brinton Perera, *Descent to the Goddess – A Way of Initiation for Women*, Inner City Books 1981, p.11.

(13) Made all the more poignant by the fact that there is no 'legitimate' word for it, *gynocide* is defined by Mary Daly in *Webster's First New Intergalactic Wickedary of the English Language*, The Women's Press Ltd. 1988, as 'the fundamental intent of global patriarchy: planned, institutionalized spiritual and bodily destruction of women; the use of deliberate systematic measures (such as killing, bodily or mental injury, unliveable conditions, prevention of births), which are calculated to bring about the destruction of women as a political and cultural force, the eradication of Female/Bio-logical religion and language, and ultimately the extermination of the Race of Women and all

Elemental being; the master model of genocide; paradigm for the systematic destruction of any racial, political, or cultural group.'

(14) 'East Coker' in T.S.Eliot, *Four Quartets* from *Collected Poems 1909-1962*, pp.200, 201 and 204.

STAGE 5: OPENING

(1) Ken Wilber.

(2) Stephen Levine, *A Gradual Awakening*, Rider 1980, p.38.

(3) Rescuing, in the guise of 'doing good', can operate the same way on a wider scale *viz.*: "I received a letter from my teacher in India, and he said, 'After a period of a few months doing the *sadhana* you're doing, you will be able to read other people's minds.' I thought, 'Oh, wow, I sure don't want that because that's the last thing a huge ego like me needs. Then when I thought it all up, I said, 'Well, why didn't the guys do it who are ready?' It gave me pause, like maybe they know something I don't know, you know? Maybe in my zeal to do good I'm going to... I started to see that I was upsetting balances in the universe that would be very destructive if I didn't understand it all." *Doing Your Own Being*, Ram Dass, London: Neville Spearman Ltd. 1970, pp. 89-90.

(4) Yogananda tells the touching story of a young pet deer that nearly died from overfeeding and which he kept from death through fervent prayer. The deer appeared to him in a dream and said: 'You are holding me back. Please let me go; let me go!'
'All right,' I answered in the dream.
   I awoke immediately, and cried out, 'Boys, the deer is dying!' I ran to the corner of the room where I had placed the pet. It made a last effort to rise, stumbled toward me, then dropped at my feet, dead' – *Autobiography of a Yogi*, Paramhansa Yogananda, Rider 1950, pp.211-212.

(5) Marcus Toyne, *Involved In Mankind: The Life and Message of Vivekananda*, Ramakrishna Vedanta Centre 1983, pp.39-40.

STAGE 6: POWER & SURRENDER

(1) Ram Dass, *Doing Your Own Being*, London: Neville Spearman Ltd. 1970, p.69.

(2) D.E.Harding quoted in *On Being One-Self – A Resource Book of Modern Experiments and Traditional Wisdom*, ed. Anne Seward, Shollond Publications, p.47.

(3) Ramana Maharshi, *The Teachings of Ramana Maharshi*, Ed. A. Osborne, Rider 1962, p.127.

(4) Jack Kornfield, *A Path with a Heart*, New York: Bantam 1993, p.109.

(5) John Welwood, *Journey of the Heart*, Mandala 1991, pp.21-22.

(6) "The Tao does nothing and yet nothing is left undone.' These famous words of Lao Tzu obviously cannot be taken in their literal sense, for the principle of 'non-action' (*wu-*

wei) is not to be considered inertia, laziness, *laissez-faire*, or mere passivity. Among the several meanings of *wei* are to be, to do, to act out. It [can also mean] false, simulate, counterfeit. But in the context of Taoist writings it quite clearly means forcing, meddling and artifice – in other words, trying to act against the grain of *li* [the natural order of Tao]." – Alan Watts in collaboration with Al Chung-Liang Huang, *TAO: The Watercourse Way*, Penguin 1979, pp.75-76.

(7) Lao Tzu, *Tao Te Ching*, trans. Gia-Fu Feng and Jane English, Wildwood House 1973, chapter 48, with notes in brackets from *The Rider Encyclopaedia of Eastern Philosophy and Religion*, Rider 1989, p.421.

(8) C. G. Jung, from the foreword to *The I Ching or Book of Changes*, The Richard Wilhelm Translation rendered into English by Cary F. Baynes, Routledge & Kegan Paul 1968, p.*xxiv*.

(9) Johann Wolfgang von Goethe quoted in Oscar Browning, *Goethe: His Life and Writings*, USA: Haskell House Publishers 1972.

(10) Kahlil Gibran, *The Prophet*, Heinemann: London 1974, pp. 16-19.

(11) Sylvia Brinton Perera, *Descent to the Goddess – A Way of Initiation for Women*, Inner City Books 1981, p.55.

(12) From the article 'Shakespeare and Religion' by Aldous Huxley in Julian Huxley, *Aldous Huxley 1894-1963: A Memorial Tribute*, Chatto and Windus, p.174.

(13) Carlos Castaneda, *The Fire From Within*, Black Swan 1985, p.27.

(14) *Ibid.*, p.46.

(15) Thich Nhat Hanh, *Peace Is Every Step*, Bantam Books 1991, p.27 and p.29.

(16) Thomas Merton, *The Climate of Monastic Prayer*, Continuum International 1981.

(17) 'Diamond Sutra', quoted in *On Being One-Self – A Resource Book of Modern Experiments and Traditional Wisdom*, ed. Anne Seward, Shollond Publications, p.27. Buddha's *Diamond Sutra* is, 'sharp like a diamond that cuts away all unnecessary conceptualisation and brings one to the further shore of enlightenmen'. – *The Rider Encyclopaedia of Eastern Philosophy and Religion*, Rider 1989, p.91.

(18) *The Upanishads*, trans. Juan Mascaro, Penguin Books 1965.

STAGE 7: EXPANSION

(1) Marianne Williamson, *A Return to Love*, HarperCollins: New York 1992, quoted by Nelson Mandela in his 1994 Inaugural Speech.

(2) Karlfried Graf Durckheim, *Absolute Living – The Otherworldly in the World and the Path to Maturity*, Arkana 1992.

(3) Sri Nisargadatta Maharaj quoted in *On Being One-Self – A Resource Book of Modern Experiments and Traditional Wisdom*, ed. Anne Seward, Shollond Publications, p.53.

(4) Karlfried Graf Durckheim, *Absolute Living – The Otherworldly in the World and the Path to Maturity*, Arkana 1992, p.119.

(5) Joseph Campbell, *The Power of Myth*, Doubleday 1988, p.55.

(6) Elaine Pagels, *The Gnostic Gospels*, New York: Random House 1979, p.74.

(7) Rainer Maria Rilke, *Letters to a Young Poet*, W.W.Norton & Co. 1934.

(8) Roshi Jiyu Kennett, *Zen is Eternal Life*, Dharma Publishing 1976, p.51.

(9) James 1.5, *The Holy Bible*, New International Version, New York International Bible Society 1978, p.1083.

(10) Alan Watts, *OM: Creative Meditations*, Celestial Arts 1980, p.93.

(11) Kabir, *Songs of Kabir*, trans. Rabindranath Tagore, Samuel Weiser 1977, p.133.

(12) From 'The Baby and Its Toy' in *Pictorial Parables of Sri Ramakrishna*, Advaita Ashrama Publications, p.19.

STAGE 8: ONENESS WITH THE SELF

(1) "[Black Elk] said, 'The central city, the central mountain, is Harney Peak in South Dakota, but the central mountain is everywhere.' This text says god is an intelligible sphere whose centre is everywhere and circumference nowhere." – Joseph Campbell, *This business of the gods…*, in conversation with Fraser Boa, Windrose Films Ltd.1989, p.126.

(2) Chuang Tzu, *The Book of Chuang Tzu*, trans. Martin Palmer with Elizabeth Breuilly, Chang Wai Ming and Jay Ramsay, Arkana 1996.

(3) Arnold Mindell interviewed by Sarida Brown, 'In the Fire of Worldwork', *Caduceus* magazine, issue 33.

(4) Johann Wolfgang von Goethe, *West-oestlicher Divan*, Deutscher Taschenbuch Verlag (DTV) 1997.

(5) Sri Krishna Prem, *The Yoga of the Bhagavat Gita*, Element Books 1990.

(6) *Ibid*.

(7) St. John of the Cross quoted in Aldous Huxley, *The Perennial Philosophy*, Harper Colophon 1970, p.105.

(8) *Ibid*. p.106.

(9) Sri Ramakrishna.

(10) T.S. Eliot, 'East Coker' from *Four Quartets*, *Collected Poems 1909-1962*, p.200-204.

(11) St John of the Cross, *The Dark Night of the Soul*, trans. Kurt F. Reinhardt, Frederick Ungar Publishing Co. 1957.

(12) Joseph Campbell quoting 'La Queste del Saint Graal' in *An Open Life*, Joseph Campbell in conversation with Michael Toms, Harper and Row 1989, p.73.

(13) *The Bhagavad Gita*, trans. Eknath Easwaran, Arkana 1985, p.63.

(14) Dogen Zenji, 'Fukanzazengi' (Zazen Rules) in Roshi Jiyu Kennett, *Zen Is Eternal Life*, Dharma Publishing 1976, p.287.

(15) C.G.Jung, *VII Sermones ad Mortuos (The Seven Sermons to the Dead)*, trans. H.G.Baynes, Robinson and Watkins Ltd. 1967, pp.21, 23 and 24.

(16) Galway Kinnell, 'St. Francis and the Sow' in *Fifty Years of American Poetry*, New York: Dell Publishing 1984, p.165.

(17) Ramakrishna quoted in *Ramakrishna: Prophet of New India*, trans. Swami Nikhilananda, Rider 1951.

(18) 'Guarding the One' – Talks given by Shi Fu on the first two evenings of the Ch'an retreat in April 1989', in *New Ch'an Forum*, No.1 Summer 1990, p.8.

(19) Thomas Merton, *New Seeds of Contemplation*, New Directions 1974.

(20) Deena Metzger, 'Return' in *The Axis Mundi Poems*, Los Angeles: Jazz Press 1981.

STAGE 9: RETURNING TO THE SOURCE

(1) Krishnamurti, *The Second Penguin Krishnamurti Reader*, ed. Mary Lutyens, Penguin 1970, p.164.

(2) Thomas Merton, *The Way of Chuang Tzu*, New Directions 1975.

(3) Quoted in Giorgio de Santillana and Hertha van Dechend, *Hamlet's Mill*, David R. Godine Inc. 1977, p.348.

(4) From the 'Kena Upanishad' in *The Upanishads*, trans. Juan Mascaro, Penguin Books 1965, p.51.

(5) 'The Empty Boat' in Thomas Merton, *The Way of Chuang Tzu*, New Directions 1965, p.114.

(6) 'Kasan Sweated', *Zen Flesh, Zen Bones*, Compiled by Paul Reps, Pelican 1971, p.63.

(7) Robert A. Johnson, *Transformation: Understanding the Three Levels of Masculine Consciousness*, HarperCollins 1991, p.59.

(8) Joseph Campbell, *The Power of Myth*, Doubleday 1988, p.67.

(9) Rumi, *Whoever Brought Me Here Will Have To Take Me Home*, trans. Coleman Barks with John Moyne, Arkana 1998, p.45.

(10) Hazrat Inayat Khan, (trans. from the German) quoted in *The Healing Power of Illness*, Thorwald Dethlefsen, Element 1990, p.268.

(11) Jesus, 'The Gnostic Gospel of Thomas', Log.22 in Elaine Pagels, *The Gnostic Gospels*, New York: Random House 1979.

(12) Ramakrishna quoted in *The Bhagavad Gita*, trans. Juan Mascaro, Penguin 1962, pp.19-20. Compare this passage: 'The Absolute Truth is realised in three phases of understanding by the knower of the Absolute Truth, and all of them are identical. Such phases of the Absolute Truth are expressed as Brahman, Paramatma and Bhagavan'. – A.C. Bhaktivedanta Swami Prabhupada, *Bhagavad-Gita – As It Is*, Bhaktivedanta Book Trust 1883, p.75.

(13) Compare the I-Thou relationship in Martin Buber, *I and Thou*, T. and T. Clark 1970.

STAGE 10: FREEDOM

(1) Frances G. Wickes, *The Inner World of Choice*, Sigo Press: Boston 1988, pp.15 and 20.

(2) The philosopher of Advaita-Vedanta, Shankara (788-820 AD), 'Vivekacudamani', vss. 427-30, quoted in *The Spiritual Heritage of India*, Swami Prabhavananda, Vedanta Press 1979, p.264.

(3) Being unseen is also a defensive position in Stages 1 and 2 – *Seeing Yourself As You Are* and *Developing Faith* – of the spiritual journey. The challenge for such people is to allow themselves to be fully seen. I have known people who confuse the defensive position with holiness. Introverts get attracted to the hermit's life but in a death-like way.

(4) Sri Nisargadatta Maharaj, *I Am That*, The Acorn Press 1973.

(5) *A Course in Miracles*, Arkana 1985, p.466.

(6) From Lao Tzu, *Tao Te Ching*, trans. Gia-Fu Feng and Jane English, Wildwood House 1973, chapter 38. There is a remark, which echoes this, attributed to the artist Edgar Degas: 'Only when he no longer knows what he is doing does the painter do good things'.

(7) Da Free John, *The Knee of Listening*, Dawn Horse Press 1972, p.271.

(8) D.T. Suzuki.

(9) Sylvia Brinton Perera, *Descent to the Goddess – A Way of Initiation for Women*, Inner City Books 1981, p.59.

(10) 'Buddha's Zen', *Zen Flesh, Zen Bones*, Compiled by Paul Reps, Penguin 1971, p.86.

(11) 'The Vedanta Philosophy' in Swami Vivekananda, *The Complete Works of Swami Vivekananda*, India: Advaita Ashrama 1984, pp.364-365.

(12) Joseph Campbell, *The Power of Myth*, Doubleday 1988, p.110.

(13) Georg Feuerstein, *Holy Madness*, Arkana 1992, p.68. The quote within the passage is from Bhagwan Shree Rajneesh, *Tantra: The Supreme Understanding*, Poona, India: Rajneesh Foundation 1975.

(14) Martin Buber, *Hasidism*, New York: Philosophical Library 1948.

(15) William Johnston, *Christian Zen*, Fordham University Press 1977.

(16) Dogen Zenji, 'Fukanzazengi' (Zazen Rules) in Roshi Jiyu Kennett, *Zen Is Eternal Life*, Dharma Publishing 1976, p.287

(17) Sri Nisargadatta Maharaj, *Prior to Consciousness – Talks with Sri Nisargadatta Maharaj*, ed. Jean Dunn, The Acorn Press 1990.

(18) The Venerable Sangharakshita, *The Thousand Petalled Lotus*, William Heinemann, p.197-8.

(19) Dom John Main, *Moment of Christ*, Darton, Longman and Todd, quoted in *The Fire of Silence and Stillness – An Anthology of Quotations for the Spiritual Journey*, ed. Paul Harris, Darton, Longman and Todd 1995, p.111.

WORKSHOPS AND COURSES

If you would like information about workshops and courses led by Richard Harvey, including *The Flight of Consciousness – A Contemporary Map for the Spiritual Journey*, based on the ideas and exercises in this book, please write: Richard Harvey, c/o Ashgrove Publishing, 55 Richmond Avenue, London N1 0LX

ACKNOWLEDGEMENTS

Acknowledgement is made for the use of the following: lines from 'East Coker' from *Four Quartets* in *Collected Poems 1909-1962* © T.S. Eliot, 1963, reprinted by permission of Faber & Faber Ltd. and for 'A suitcase full of dust' in *Love Poems*, reprinted by permission of HarperCollins Publishers Ltd, © Brian Patten, 1992.

INDEX

Published in Great Britain by

ASHGROVE PUBLISHING
an imprint of
HOLLYDATA PUBLISHERS LTD

55 Richmond Avenue
London N1 0LX

© 2002 Richard Harvey

ISBN 1-85398-141-9

First Edition

Book Design by Brad Thompson
Cover Illustration by
Printed and bound in Malta by Interprint